RAND NATIONAL SECURITY RESEARCH DIVISION

Rethinking Coordination of Services to Refugees in Urban Areas

Managing the Crisis in Jordan and Lebanon

Shelly Culbertson, Olga Oliker, Ben Baruch, Ilana Blum

Prepared for the U.S. Department of State

For more information on this publication, visit www.rand.org/t/RR1485

Library of Congress Cataloging-in-Publication Data is available for this publication.
ISBN: 978-0-8330-9446-9

Published by the RAND Corporation, Santa Monica, Calif.

Cover image: UNHCR/S.Hoibak

Preface

The Syrian civil war has displaced about half of Syria's population; many have fled either within Syria or abroad. Syria's neighbors—particularly Lebanon, Turkey, Jordan, Iraq, and Egypt—have, to varying degrees, opened their borders to the refugees, and the international aid community has responded with assistance. How well is this assistance working, and how effective is the humanitarian assistance community (a wide variety of donors, host-country governments, United Nations agencies, nongovernmental organizations, and other stakeholders) in providing services to refugees? This report analyzes coordination of provision of services to Syrian refugees in Jordan and Lebanon and provides recommendations on improving coordination strategies and practices. Because the vast majority of Syrian refugees live in urban areas (as has been increasingly the case in refugee crises overall), not camps, this report focuses on coordination of aid to refugees in urban and other non-camp settings. The report should be of particular interest to donors, policymakers, and practitioners concerned with the provision of assistance in the Syrian refugee crisis and in other urban refugee crises as well.

This research was sponsored by the Bureau of Population, Refugees, and Migration within the U.S. Department of State and conducted within the International Security and Defense Policy Center of the RAND National Security Research Division (NSRD). NSRD conducts research and analysis on defense and national security topics for the U.S. and allied defense, foreign policy, homeland security, and intelligence communities and foundations and other nongovernmental organizations that support defense and national security analysis.

For more information on the International Security and Defense Policy Center, see www.rand.org/nsrd/ndri/centers/isdp or contact the director (contact information is provided on the web page).

Contents

Figures and Tables

Figures

Tables

Summary

Background, Purpose, and Report Contributions

The 4.7 million Syrian refugees in Turkey, Lebanon, Jordan, Iraq, and Egypt are straining host countries' capacity to absorb refugees into public services, housing, and labor markets. United Nations (UN) funding appeals to support this are at unprecedented levels; in 2015, it was $5.5 billion. Donor commitments have not kept pace with the UN appeals for funding; as of the end of 2015, the UN had received only $2.8 billion of the $5.5 billion it had requested for the Syrian refugee crisis. While European countries also are now facing the challenges posed by half a million Syrians seeking refuge, the countries of the Middle East have opened their doors to numbers that are several multiples greater, with concomitant strains on their resources and societies. Not only is more money needed, new solutions also are needed.

In addition to the sheer size of the crisis, its attributes further complicate the situation. Unlike some past crises, this crisis is largely urban, with most refugees not living in refugee camps, but in host communities. The prevalence of the refugees in host communities instead of camps is a result both of strong preferences on the part of many refugees to not live in camps if they have the option and of new guidance from the UN High Commissioner for Refugees (UNHCR) promoting host communities as a more durable solution for the refugees than camps. In addition, the government of Lebanon has decided to not offer camps as a settlement option (as Palestinian camps from 1967 are occupied to this day). As a result, models of assistance and assistance coordination that allow the humanitarian community to provide for the refugees' needs in camps are not as relevant here. The Syrian refugee crisis thus far is also one of refugees fleeing from a middle-income country in crisis and going primarily to other middle-income countries. The capacities of both the host-country governments and the refugees themselves are greater than in other recent refugee circumstances, where refugees have left failing states to seek safety in other failing or impoverished states.

Funded by the U.S. State Department's Bureau of Population, Refugees, and Migration (PRM), this report focuses on identifying ways to improve coordination of the Syrian refugee response in urban areas in Jordan and Lebanon, particularly in the legal, employment, shelter, water and sanitation, health, and education sectors.

This report makes several contributions to the existing literature on this topic. First, it assesses the management model of a complex emergency response in urban areas in middle-income countries; most existing literature about humanitarian responses focuses on camps in weak states. Second, it brings together views of a broad spectrum of stakeholders to provide a comprehensive, multidimensional analysis of management of the Syrian refugee crisis in Jordan and Lebanon in particular; we are not aware of other work that does this specifically for these two countries. Third, this report presents a new framework for planning, evaluating, and managing refugee crises in urban settings, both in the Syrian refugee crisis as well as other such situations going forward. Fourth, it provides concrete recommendations for how to better support the needs of Syrian urban refugees in Jordan and Lebanon and for how to rethink refugee-assistance coordination around the world for improved effectiveness in the future.

This report drew on multiple methods: a literature review; interviews in Jordan and Lebanon with officials from donor countries, UN agencies, host governments, and nongovernmental organizations (NGOs); telephone interviews with international experts; and focus groups with refugees.

Evolving Models of Urban Refugee Responses

With refugee crises around the world increasingly involving refugees settling in urban areas, the international assistance community is reassessing its approaches to refugee assistance in humanitarian emergencies in two important ways.

1. **From camps to urban areas.** Response models based on helping refugees in camps are not viable in urban areas. In urban areas, many services to refugees rely less on aid agencies (such as the UN and international NGOs) and more on line ministries, municipal authorities, the private sector, police, national civil society actors, and the refugees themselves. Furthermore, refugees adapt best when they can become self-reliant, gain employment, and meet many of their own needs and the needs of their families.
2. **From humanitarianism and development to resilience.** Relatedly, because refugees are interspersed with local communities, the average duration of a protracted refugee crisis is 25 years, and local authorities are critical to any response, emergency humanitarian responses for refugees must be linked and aligned with host-country development plans. But while the recognition of these realities is an important first step, effective new approaches have been slow to develop.

In Jordan and Lebanon, multiple stakeholders argued that "humanitarian" responses had not achieved desired results in meeting the shorter- and longer-term needs of refugees in urban areas, and national development plans had yet to integrate the needs of the refugees and their host communities. The crisis grew to the extent that it affected overall development agendas in these countries, straining resources and degrading infrastructure.

With growing recognition that the refugee crisis was becoming protracted, the UN-sponsored 2015 Regional Refugee and Resilience Plan (3RP) for the Syrian refugee crisis attempted to combine a refugee humanitarian response with host-country development considerations, using the term “resilience” to blend the two approaches. However, while it was important to recognize the need for a new model, consensus is lacking about what “resilience” actually means in concrete terms.

We propose a framework that recognizes that there are tensions between approaches and perspectives in five different (if somewhat overlapping) areas. Our findings suggest that there are no single right answers to these issues (which we call “approach areas”), regardless of the circumstance. We propose the approach areas as a checklist to consider when planning and evaluating coordination of health, education, shelter, and the other sectors in refugee responses. The approach areas are:

- **Short- versus medium-term planning.** Should planning be for a temporary response (one to two years) or a sustainable response (at least ten years)?
- **Parallel versus integrated services.** Should UN agencies and NGOs provide separate, parallel public services to the refugees, or should governments integrate refugees into their public services for their citizens?
- **Internationally versus nationally lead.** Should international entities (donors, UN agencies, NGOs) lead policies, or should national governmental entities lead policies?
- **Funding to international entities versus funding to national entities.** Should donor funding flow to UN agencies and international NGOs for public services or to governments and local NGOs? Should donor funding be directed toward entities that are providing the public services?
- **Focus on refugees versus on host communities.** Should policies and programs be directed at the refugees as a separate group or directed at the communities in which they reside?

An Overview of Coordination in Jordan and Lebanon

An internationally led refugee response helped meet needs for many refugees early in the Syrian crisis, no doubt saving lives. To do this, it relied on coordination mechanisms that had been used in other refugee responses. Yet, in both Jordan and Lebanon, the countries discussed in this report, these involved the establishment of an expensive and time-consuming coordination structure, which was based on approaches used in previous crises elsewhere. As the crisis continued, efforts to work within that structure have increasingly been characterized by tensions among the UN agencies and between the governments and the international assistance community. Moreover, the approach has been blamed for marginalizing the refugees themselves and raised questions regarding how effectively donor money is being spent. Meanwhile, many public services in Jordan and Lebanon are now deeply overburdened, and aid money for parallel services provided by the international community is dwindling.

These issues have led to reconsideration of the coordination model in place and the roles and responsibilities of the major stakeholders. There are multiple elements to coordination: participants, coordination structures, budgeting and money flows, and information, considered below.

Participants. There are multiple participants, and thus coordination roles and responsibilities, in the refugee crises in Jordan and Lebanon. They include the governments, UN agencies, donors, NGOs, the private sector, the refugees themselves, and host communities. Each of these entities brings unique value to the response, as well as their own specific limitations. They also have different priorities, which has made it difficult to agree on goals and strategies for how to coordinate services.

Our interviews indicate that what might at first appear to be coordination problems are actually driven by fundamental differences between stakeholders regarding what should be done, by whom, and for whom. These fundamental differences are about divergent views on the approach areas: over short- or long-term planning for the refugee crisis, whether refugee services should be managed by the international community or integrated with national efforts, whether leadership resides with international or national actors, who receives the donor funding, and whether efforts aid only the refugees or include the host communities. These differences manifest in what seem to others to be ineffectiveness, inefficiency, and sometimes even obstinance. As a result, the crisis has been characterized by failure to agree on goals within the governments, among the UN agencies, and between the international and national response communities. This is not a matter of coordination, but a matter of different institutional cultures and competing priorities.

Coordination structures. The development of coordination structures followed similar patterns in Jordan and Lebanon. In the beginning of the crisis, UNHCR took leadership of coordination, involving governments, other UN agencies, and NGOs. In 2014–2015, the governments of both Jordan and Lebanon stepped forward to exert more influence and control over coordination, demanding more consideration for addressing host-community needs alongside refugee needs.

There are both strengths and challenges with existing coordination structures. Strengths include integrating resilience or stabilization goals into a refugee-coordination structure, increasing government leadership, and meeting many needs quickly. Challenges and gaps include unclear responsibilities among UN agencies, differences between governments and UN agencies, diffusion of responsibility and limited capacity within host-nation governments, multiple time and resource-intensive coordination structures, little coordination among donors about policy priorities, insular coordination among the international community, misaligned incentives between governments and NGOs, and little coordination with refugees.

Budgeting and money flows. While the report does not provide a full budget analysis, it considers how budgets are coordinated, as outlined below.

How budgets are developed and prioritized. The 2015 3RP budget appeal brought together the aid community and governments to link budget requirements for the refugee response and support for local needs. However, the 3RP budget was based on a coordinated consensus of the positions of governments and 200 international and national partners and not on systematic needs assessments or options appraisals. Some budget items appear to be for parallel NGO-provided services that lack plans for local authorities to take on these roles in time. Others look like host-country development requests, independent of the refugee response.

How budget information is tracked. In both countries, there are gaps in clearly accounting for funding sources, destinations, and amounts. This is due to the many donors, implementers, and recipients, along with few centralized ways to aggregate their activities. As a result, donors are frustrated that governments cannot report how much money they have received from various sources, while governments are unhappy that they lack a complete picture of how aid funds from around the world are being spent in their countries.

The cost of coordination. Too much funding is spent on the coordination system itself, specifically in (1) staff time spent in coordination, (2) budgets passing through multiple agencies, and (3) high overhead rates.

Where the money goes. Of the $5.5 billion from the UN-led funding appeal, $1 billion would have been allocated to the governments and $4.5 billion to the UN system and NGOs. Such allocations do not reflect the responsibility governments also have for providing health care, water and sanitation, and education services. At the same time, donors often prefer to route funding through UN agencies and NGOs rather than the governments, for reasons that include mandates for humanitarian funding to be spent via UN agencies; concerns about accountability; and, in Lebanon's case, politics.

Where the money comes from. Sources of funding for the refugee response include host governments, donors, and the refugees themselves. The $2.8 billion of the 2015 3RP that has actually been funded comes to approximately $660 per refugee per year, less than $2 per day. This is far from enough to meet the needs of daily life. Yet, in Jordan and Lebanon, refugees are not allowed to work unless they obtain rarely given work permits. Their labor is not considered as a possible source of funding for dealing with the crisis.

Information. A number of innovative information practices have been developed or used in Jordan and Lebanon for the Syrian refugee crisis, including new uses of data and new information-sharing tools. Yet, while information sharing among the aid community has been innovative, the flow of information to Syrian refugees has been insufficient from their perspective. In focus groups, a majority of the Syrian refugees said that they have a hard time getting information from or communicating with service providers. Referrals of refugees to specialized services are not systematic; while NGOs would prefer a comprehensive referral database tool, such a tool would pose significant privacy and security concerns. Interviewees believed that there is "no good way of evaluating aid," due to the dearth of useful data about budgets, programs, and recipients.

Recommendations

Based on this analysis, we propose a number of recommendations, targeted to donor governments, host governments, international organizations, and others.

Create a U.S.-led "Contact Group" for the Syrian refugee response. Political and diplomatic leadership is needed to address the Syrian refugee crisis. As the United States has been the largest donor in the refugee response (more than the next three largest donors combined), there are opportunities for greater policy leadership by the U.S. State Department as well. Akin to an approach during the Balkan wars, during which the U.S. State Department initiated and led the "Contact Group" (a six-country leadership group), we recommend that the U.S. State Department initiate and lead a Contact Group of leading nations for the Syrian refugee crisis. The Contact Group could integrate resources and policies into realistic funded plans, develop common priorities and solutions, and leverage the significant donor funding to help host governments implement sound policy solutions.

Develop a planning process for the refugee responses in Jordan and Lebanon that has a ten-year outlook. The Syrian refugee situation will likely span at least a decade, yet planning for it has been mainly short-term and reactive. The Contact Group should therefore work with UNHCR to develop a planning process that assumes a ten-year refugee response in Jordan, Lebanon, and other host countries. While creating medium-term plans is a challenge for both governments and most of the agencies involved, at the least, planning should assume that a ten-year horizon is possible, even if plan specifics are only detailed for a shorter term. Given the extensive unmet needs among the refugees, the continuing nature of the crisis, current budgets that primarily support the UN system and international NGOs rather than Jordanian and Lebanese institutions, and the low proportion of the UN donor request for 2015 that was funded, a new set of prioritized plans is needed, with accompanying budgets. Furthermore, for the United States, PRM and the United States Agency for International Development should collaborate on joint plans.

Create a funding plan with a ten-year vision in parallel with other funding sources. Stable and efficient funding and financial management are necessary to meet the needs of the Syrian refugees and their host communities. As part of the "Contact Group" process, we recommend that the U.S. support planning with a ten-year funding vision and coordinate with other key donors to do likewise, in exchange for the development of prioritized plans and budgets, as well as host government policy solutions on sensitive issues such as registration and employment. Aid money alone will not be enough to cover the needs of the 4.7 million Syrian refugees; this will require other sources as well. In particular, employment policies are needed to enable the Syrians to support themselves and pay taxes for the public services that they rely on. Creative private-sector funding sources, such as public-private partnerships, bonds, enterprise funds, and interest-free loans, should also be explored.

Base new plans in Jordan and Lebanon for each sector on needs assessments using the approach areas as a framework. For each sector in each country (this report focuses on the legal; employment; shelter; water, sanitation, and hygiene; health; and education sectors), donors and aid providers should take a systematic approach to defining the balance among short- versus medium-term actions, parallel versus integrated services, an international versus national lead, funding to international entities versus funding to national entities, and programming focused on refugees versus on host communities. The criteria suggested in this report can help think through those strategies.

Build capacity of governments, municipalities, national civil society, and the private sectors so they can take greater roles. Over time, management of public services to the refugees in Jordan and Lebanon will need to transition to less direct management by UN agencies and international NGOs and toward more management from national and municipal governments, civil society actors, the refugees themselves, and the private sector. Therefore, donors should invest in building capacity of these entities, with additional investment in national public-service operations, infrastructure, and institutional systems, as well as targeted inclusion of local NGOs in international forums.

Invest in government financial-accountability systems. To promote confidence in transparency and accountability of financial management of the governments of Jordan and Lebanon and thereby enable direct donor funding of government-provided integrated services, donors should invest in government financial-accountability systems, such as in third-party auditing, accounting, or Project Management Units embedded in ministries (similar to approaches used by the foreign-aid agency, Millennium Challenge Corporation).

Streamline the international coordination structures and funding channels in Jordan and Lebanon. Furthermore, because donor funding is currently being inefficiently spent on a complex coordination system, donors (with U.S. leadership) should streamline the international coordination structures and funding channels in Jordan and Lebanon, reducing reliance on large bureaucracies and channeling funding directly to service providers, with fewer contracting pass-throughs. Furthermore, coordination itself (among UN agencies, NGOs, and governments) should be refocused from frequent tactical interactions to collaborative strategy and planning.

Establish and maintain clear UN agency roles and responsibilities. Furthermore, to reduce overlapping roles, competition, and expensive duplication of UN agencies in Jordan and Lebanon, the UN Inter-Agency Standing Committee should *define clear* responsibilities among the UN agencies present in each country and develop a mechanism for resolving coordination difficulties among UN agencies.

Include refugees in coordination of the refugee response and improve communication to refugees. While refugees have been the recipients of assistance, they have largely not been included in the management of the response to help them. New management structures should include refugees in coordination of the refugee response, by means of refugee advisory groups, community-based hubs, and hiring refugees on programs that work with refugees. Communication to refugees should be improved through an online information hub, television announcements, apps, and brochures.

Roll out a municipality prioritization and coordination effort to meet local needs. We recommend a donor-funded program to convene leadership from municipalities and representatives of the refugees who reside in those municipalities to develop a priority list of investments to enable communities to manage the presence of the refugees. Finding ways to meet community needs may also ameliorate some of the tensions between the host communities and refugees.

Engage the private sector in coordination in relevant areas as another way to transition management to local actors. As both Lebanon and Jordan have thriving private sectors and functioning markets, there are opportunities for donors, UN agencies, and governments to find creative or more-efficient ways of addressing some of the medium-term problems by engaging the private sector. Ways of doing so include involving private-sector representatives in UN-led sector working groups, soliciting private-sector solutions through UN or donor tenders, exploring public-private partnerships with governments for building needed public infrastructure, or engaging private-sector providers in expanding education and health care.

Seek win-win opportunities that coordinate both refugee needs and host-country development goals in program design, rather than focusing solely on the refugees as a separate group. Examples include investing in infrastructure expansion for host countries, hiring refugees as staff on refugee-service projects, developing standards for the refugee response that also benefit the host community, and conducting a labor-market study about how refugees can contribute to economies.

Conclusion: Risks of the Status Quo

Despite dedicated people working around the clock to help, the current refugee response in Jordan and Lebanon is not meeting needs in education, health care, shelter, water and sanitation, and livelihoods. Although the war in Syria has already lasted years, it is difficult for many stakeholders in Jordan and Lebanon to publicly acknowledge that the refugee crisis and its effects will continue longer than anticipated. This is exacerbated by competing visions about the right courses of action and resource constraints. The recommendations presented in this report will be difficult to implement: They involve changing funding models, working relationships, roles and responsibilities, and planning time frames, all in the midst of crisis.

But these challenges are outweighed by the tremendous risks and costs posed by the status quo. Failure to improve the effectiveness of the management and coordination of the refugee response means a much broader failure. This includes, first of all, five million refugees who cannot meet their basic needs. This, in turn, creates longer-term economic and societal risks, which may last generations, given the educational gaps that face at least half of the refugee children and the lack of opportunities for refugee (and host community) youth. The inadequacy of the response in Jordan and Lebanon is partly responsible for the further waves of migration to Europe. Second, Jordan and Lebanon are under strain, as their governments are providing what they can in the way of education, health care, and more to the refugees without adequate donor funding, degrading previously robust public services. In time, this could threaten stability in those countries, as host communities become ever more frustrated with the effects on their own circumstances, as demonstrated by public protests in Beirut in 2015 over overburdened sanitation systems that were no longer able to collect garbage. Third, continuing reliance on outdated approaches to the refugee response creates and perpetuates expensive and ineffective parallel services. By increasing costs, it contributes further to difficulties in the needs regarding education, health care, sanitation, and more. Investment in internationally managed services now, as opposed to national services, will not leave the capacity behind in the future. In addition, creation of separate facilities for education, health care, and more has the potential to further divide societies that are ever more fragile because of the civil war and refugee crisis.

While current models for the refugee response have gone a long way in meeting some needs, they will not be able to expand services as quickly as needed to as many people as needed, and sustain those services into the future. This is why change is needed.

Acknowledgments

We would like to thank Maria Rowan, our sponsor at the U.S. State Department's Bureau of Population, Refugees, and Migration, for her project guidance and facilitation, as well as her numerous helpful comments and her shepherding of this project through to completion. We would like to thank Seth Jones, director of RAND's International Security and Defense Policy Center, for his review, and our two formal peer reviewers, Amb. Charles Ries, vice president of International, a unit at the RAND Corporation, and Elizabeth Ferris, senior research associate at Georgetown University and non-resident senior fellow in foreign policy at the Brookings Institution, for their helpful feedback. We would also like to recognize the generous support of RAND's Center for Middle East Public Policy. The authors are grateful to the many individuals in the government of Jordan, government of Lebanon, donor governments, UN agencies, and NGOs for participation in interviews, sharing documents and data and contributing their time and insights to help us better understand the coordination of the refugee response in Jordan and Lebanon. We are particularly grateful to Syrian refugees who participated in our focus groups and to the NGOs who arranged our focus groups in Lebanon (International Medical Corps, Relief International, and International Rescue Committee) and Jordan (International Medical Corps, Danish Refugee Council, and CARE). We would also like to thank Michelle Horner for her support in preparing this document for publication.

Abbreviations

3RP	Regional Refugee and Resilience Plan
EU	European Union
GNI	gross national income
ICRC	International Committee of the Red Cross
JRP	Jordan Response Plan
LCRP	Lebanon Crisis Response Plan
MEHE	Ministry of Education and Higher Education (in Lebanon)
MOPIC	Ministry of Planning and International Cooperation (in Jordan)
MOSA	Ministry of Social Affairs (in Lebanon)
MOU	memorandum of understanding
NGO	nongovernmental organization
NRC	Norwegian Refugee Council
PRM	U.S. State Department's Bureau of Population, Refugees, and Migration
UN	United Nations
UNDP	United Nations Development Programme

UNESCO	United Nations Educational, Scientific, and Cultural Organization
UNHCR	United Nations High Commissioner for Refugees
UNICEF	United Nations Children's Emergency Fund
UNOCHA	United Nations Office of the Coordinator for Humanitarian Affairs
UNRWA	United Nations Relief and Works Agency for Palestine Refugees in the Near East
USAID	United States Agency for International Development
WASH	water, sanitation, and hygiene
WFP	United Nations World Food Programme
WHO	World Health Organization

CHAPTER ONE

Introduction

Background and Purpose

By the end of 2015, civil war in Syria had displaced half its population: 7.6 million persons internally and 4.7 million as refugees to other countries in the Middle East (United Nations High Commissioner for Refugees [UNHCR], 2016c, and United Nations Office for the Coordination of Humanitarian Affairs [UNOCHA], 2015). These numbers have grown (and continue to grow) at a remarkable rate. In June 2012, there were 78,000 Syrian refugees, a number that, as noted, grew over the next three years to 4.7 million (UNOCHA, 2012). The sheer numbers and pace of refugee flows make this refugee crisis the worst since World War II.

The numbers of refugees in the host countries of Turkey, Lebanon, Jordan, Iraq, and Egypt are so large that they are straining host countries' capacity to absorb refugees into public services, housing, and labor markets. The size of the crisis also means that refugee inflows are changing these countries' demographic balances. To provide for the large numbers of refugees, the UN donor funding appeals are at unprecedented levels—$5.5 billion for 2015 alone. Donor commitments have not kept pace with the UN appeals for funding; by the end of 2015, $2.8 billion of the UN agency appeals was funded (Financial Tracking Service, 2016). With 60 million people in the world displaced by violence by the end of 2014 (UNHCR, 2014e), there are many crises competing for donor funding. Indeed, in December 2015, UNHCR appealed for an unprecedented budget of $20.1 billion in humanitarian aid (Implementation of the Intergovernmental Sustainable Development Agenda, 2016). And while European countries are now also facing the challenges posed by half a million Syrians seeking refuge, Middle Eastern countries have opened their doors to numbers that are several times greater, with concomitant strains on their resources and societies. Not only is more money needed; new solutions are needed.

Some specific attributes of the Syrian crisis further complicate it. Unlike some past crises, this crisis is largely urban, with most refugees living in urban or rural host communities or informal tented settlements. Among Syrian refugees in Jordan, 85 percent live in host communities, not camps (UNHCR, 2014f, and Hashemite Kingdom of Jordan, Ministry of Planning and International Cooperation [MOPIC] and the UN, 2015). The government of Lebanon decided not to allow formal serviced refugee camps (Rainey, 2015). As a result, models of assistance and assistance coordination that allow the humanitarian community to provide for the refugees' needs in camps, separated from the host communities, are not as relevant here. Although this is not the only crisis in which many refugees live in host communities rather than in camps, the international community is still adapting its practices from camps to urban settings. The transition of aid from camps to urban settings means less service provisions by the international community and more support to existing government services.

Relatedly, the Syrian refugee crisis is one of refugees from a middle-income country going to other middle-income countries.[1] Capacities of both host-country governments and the refugees themselves are greater than in other crises, such as those of Afghanistan, Somalia, or south Sudan, where refugees left failing states to seek safety in other failing or impoverished states. Capacity of neighboring host countries in the Syrian refugee crisis is substantial, although very much strained by the influx of people.

---

[1] The World Bank defines a middle-income country as having gross national income (GNI, or purchasing power parity) per capita between $1,045 and $12,763. See World Bank, undated(a). Syria's GNI per capita in 2012 was $5,120. See Trading Economics, 2016, for more information.

Today, host countries and the international community struggle to meet needs. While international donors have not met fundraising goals, host countries face both financial shortages and political tensions over the presence of the refugees and the effects of large population increases on their own public services. Circumstances for the refugees are so dire that many are leaving for Europe. This creates an incentive to develop better approaches that enable donors, host countries, and UN agencies to work together to use scarce resources more effectively.

This report, funded by the U.S. State Department's Bureau of Population, Refugees, and Migration (PRM), identifies ways to improve coordination of the refugee response in urban areas of Jordan and Lebanon, the two countries with the largest ratios of refugees to host-country nationals. To do so, it analyzes coordination models, roles, and structures, with particular consideration of six sectors: legal, employment, shelter, water and sanitation, health, and education.

This report makes several contributions to the existing literature on this topic. First, it assesses the management model of a complex emergency response in urban areas in middle-income countries; most existing literature about humanitarian responses focuses on camps in weak states. Second, it brings together views of a broad spectrum of stakeholders to provide a comprehensive, multidimensional analysis of management of the Syrian refugee crisis in Jordan and Lebanon in particular; we are not aware of other work that does this specifically for these two countries. Third, this report presents a new framework for planning, evaluating, and managing refugee crises in urban settings, both in the Syrian refugee crisis as well as other such situations going forward. Fourth, it provides concrete recommendations for how to better support the needs of Syrian urban refugees in Jordan and Lebanon and for how to rethink refugee assistance coordination around the world for improved effectiveness in the future. Recommendations will be of use to national governments; the United States and other donors; the United Nations High Commissioner for Refugees (UNHCR) and other UN agencies; and other members of the assistance community.

General Overview and Context

The governments and people of Jordan and Lebanon have been generous in accepting so many people in difficult circumstances inside their borders. Throughout the Syrian civil war and refugee crisis, Jordan and Lebanon have maintained an open-border policy for Syrian refugees, although with increasing restrictions. As a result, Jordan and Lebanon now have the highest ratios of refugees to citizens in the world (Regional Refugee and Resilience Plan [3RP], 2015a). By the end of 2015, there were 630,000 officially registered Syrian refugees in Jordan, although government-sourced estimates put this number as high as 1.4 million ("Prince El-Hassan: Syrian Refugees Crisis Requires National-Level Thinking," 2014; UNHCR, 2016b; Kumar, 2015). Before the crisis in 2011, Jordan's population was 6.2 million; the influx of refugees means that 10 to 20 percent of the people now living in Jordan are Syrian refugees (World Bank, undated[b]). In Lebanon, there are 1.1 million officially registered Syrian refugees. This is almost certainly a lower number than the actual refugee count, as not all refugees register (UNHCR, 2016a). Before the crisis, Lebanon's population was 4.4 million; the influx of refugees means that 20 to 25 percent of the people living in Lebanon today are Syrian refugees.

Living mainly in cities and towns, most refugees in Jordan are concentrated in the northern provinces of Mafraq, Irbid, and Zarqa, close to the Syrian border, although many are also in Amman and dispersed elsewhere throughout the country. A minority of the refugees are living in Jordan's refugee camps, the largest of which are Zaatari (with 80,000 people in 2015) and Azraq (with 25,000) (UNHCR, 2016d, and UNHCR, undated[c]). In Lebanon, as in Jordan, most are in host communities, with the largest numbers in the Bekaa Valley, followed by Beirut. However, many refugees live in "informal tented settlements," which are effectively refugee camps—just not ones created and sanctioned by the state or international community. Indeed, the fact that camps are prohibited means that people in these settlements are prohibited from building permanent infrastructure, including sanitation facilities. This, of course, means that conditions for refugees living there are particularly difficult, service provision is even more challenging, and negative environmental effects are more likely.

From the refugee perspective, things are getting worse. Those refugees who came to Jordan or Lebanon over the past five years have exhausted their savings and are finding that their resources have dwindled due to constraints on their ability to work legally. Neither country has granted the refugees the right to work, unless they obtain a relatively expensive (and rarely obtained) work permit. There is a large informal work sector, with Syrians reputedly undercutting low-wage Jordanian and Lebanese workers, as well as high rates of child labor. This has significant implications for housing, and many live in cramped unsanitary quarters: multiple families to an apartment, in tents, in basements, or in garages. They do not have access to many public services, and international assistance has dropped. For example, food assistance to needy refugees dropped to $13 per person per month (per interviews), available only for the most vulnerable. Among school-age Syrian refugees, only 25 percent in Lebanon and 60 percent in Jordan are enrolled in a formal school (3RP, 2015b). While Lebanon has given refugees access to some public services, its largely privatized education and health care systems have made absorbing the Syrians difficult. UN funding for refugee health in Lebanon is so tight that, in most cases, only primary health care is available, but not secondary or tertiary. While, in theory, Jordan granted Syrian refugees access to the same public health and education services that it offers to citizens of Jordan, according to our focus groups with the refugees, resource shortages prevent the Syrians from fully accessing these. Moreover, Jordan began charging refugees for health services in 2014. Many refugees are caught in legal limbo: Their status is uncertain, and they and their families are unable to obtain or pay for renewal of their registrations.

From the perspective of government authorities in Jordan and Syria, the presence of the refugees is straining heavily burdened systems, and weak international burden sharing has left them in the lurch. National governments, line ministries, and municipalities must deliver services to both refugees and local citizens. But when refugees receive those services, resentment often results, particularly as many refugees are living in low-income communities that also lack for much in housing, services, and benefits. Refugees have made schools and hospitals more crowded. Their presence has driven up rents in poorer areas. Their efforts to work illegally are perceived to drive wages down and increase unemployment in an environment where it was already high. This leads to perceptions that refugees limit economic growth and reduce government spending on services for their own citizens. Resulting tensions between local residents and refugees have raised security concerns (World Bank, 2013; Abdih and Geginat, 2014; Luck, 2013). These are exacerbated by worries that violent actors may have crossed the border as part of the refugee flow.

Further coloring local responses are experiences both Jordan and Syria have had with past crises, which are closely related to ethnic tensions in those countries. At least a third (2 million people) of Jordan's population comprises Palestinian refugees and their descendants (3RP, 2015c). Jordan also accepted Iraqi refugees in the wake of conflict in that country (60,000 Iraqis remain in Jordan in 2015) (UNHCR, 2015a). In Lebanon, there are 455,000 registered Palestinian refugees and their descendants (UNRWA, 2015). Many Palestinians in both countries continue to lack full citizenship rights. Further complicating the issue is Lebanon's delicate sectarian or "confessional" balance among Christians, Sunni, Shiites, and Druze, which is the basis for the country's tenuous political settlements achieved after many years of bloody civil war. While there are no public data, some of those we interviewed estimate that 90 percent of Syrian refugees in Lebanon are Sunnis. If so, and if this population remains in Lebanon long-term, then the resulting shift in the confessional balance may have significant implications for political stability and the Lebanese settlement. For example, many of the Syrian refugees (largely Sunnis) have sought shelter in Lebanon's predominantly Shiite Bekaa Valley, raising concerns that sectarian tensions might emerge or be aggravated.

The states have differing levels of capacity. Gridlock defines Lebanon's government, in part by design, to ensure that each sectarian group gets a voice. Lebanon has not held a presidential election since 2008, when it elected Michel Suleiman. Suleiman's term expired in 2014, leaving the position empty. Effectively, the Council of Ministers governs Lebanon. Different ministries are controlled by different sectarian groups, limiting both incentive and ability to coordinate within the government. This can make it difficult to use foreign aid effectively (Moussaouri, 2015).

Jordan is a long-standing constitutional monarchy with its own challenges. Arab Spring protests in 2011 over dissatisfaction with economic opportunities for youth and demands for greater democratic participation led to changes in Jordan's constitution. Unlike other countries that experienced Arab Spring protests, Jordan remained stable through negotiations between the government and society, making incremental changes after Jordanians saw the Arab Spring chaos unleashed elsewhere. The refugee crisis has further pressed Jordan's economy and services, with King Abdullah II making an appeal for stabilization of Syria, saying Jordan is "maxed out," and that Jordan has been "let down by the international community" (Kumar, 2015).

Relations with Western countries, particularly the United States, also play a role in receiving and coordinating aid for the refugee response. Jordan and the United States have long been close partners in the Middle East, and Amman has received significant U.S. assistance, as well as assistance from other countries (Sharp, 2016). In 2015, the U.S. committed $1 billion per year in foreign assistance to Jordan through 2017. The Lebanese government, by contrast, cannot receive direct assistance from the United States (or the United Kingdom) as long as Hezbollah remains a part of its government. While the United States is providing some support to Lebanon for the refugee crisis, it is mainly indirect through UN agencies or international nongovernmental organizations (NGOs) and restricted to specifically allowed activities, such as training.

The international community, meanwhile, is struggling to keep pace with the situation. In both countries, UNHCR has taken leadership of the international response to the refugee crisis, channeling donor funds, operating camps (in Jordan), contracting with NGO partners to implement programs, and collaborating with other UN agencies with specialization in particular sectors (e.g., UN Children's Emergency Fund [UNICEF] for education or the UN World Food Programme [WFP] for food assistance). The United States has been the largest donor, followed by the United Kingdom, Kuwait, the European Union (EU), Germany, Canada, and others (3RP, 2015c). Donors have not fully funded the appeals for the Syrian refugee crisis, in part because of the growing number of displacement crises around the world that are stretching donors' contributions and because of a degree of cynicism among donors that these plans have been not properly prioritized within a realistic strategic framework.

Approach and Organization of the Report

We used multiple methods to determine how to improve responses to refugee crises. First, we reviewed policy, practical, and advocacy documents on the refugee crises in Jordan and Lebanon, as well as academic research and media reports. This literature review focused on coordination in general as well as on coordination in six sectors. Five of the sectors were identified by Syrian refugees in a survey as part of UNHCR's evaluation of its response to the crisis: shelter, water and sanitation, health, education, and employment (Crisp et al., 2013). To these, we added the legal sector, because the legal frameworks for refugees in both countries are critically important to coordination and aid provision.

Next, we conducted a select number of targeted interviews in Jordan and Lebanon (21 in Jordan and 19 in Lebanon) with officials from donor countries, UN agencies, host governments, and NGOs. In these interviews, we discussed strengths and weaknesses of refugee-response coordination, efforts to strengthen host-country systems, financing and resource allocation, public-service provision, information, and evaluation. Interviewees were selected in consultation with PRM and the U.S. embassies in Amman and Beirut. RAND developed an initial list of leading UN agencies, large donors, host-government ministries, and international and local NGOs, based on a document and Internet review of the management structure of the crisis in each country. Then, U.S. embassy officials and the RAND research team created the interview short list, selecting influential, representative, and unique stakeholders in each of the categories. In most cases, interviews were with heads or deputy heads of most of the local representations of the UN agencies with significant roles in each country, primary points of contact for the refugee crisis in a selection of host government ministries with central roles, and heads or deputy heads of several local representations of the NGOs with large roles. Stakeholders interviewed for this report therefore are intended to comprise a representative proportion (but clearly not all) of the leadership of the refugee crisis responses in Jordan and Lebanon. We spoke with a small but representative sample of international NGOs, as well as a few local NGOs. The interview protocol with questions asked is in Appendix B.

We supplemented the in-country interviews with ten more telephone interviews with external experts around the world about coordination of the refugee response. These experts were from headquarters of UN agencies, donors, and NGOs. This interview list was developed in consultation with U.S. State Department experts and expanded with recommendations from others interviewed. These interviews covered a range of sectors, agencies, and perspectives, and used the same interview protocol as the in-country interviews.

In Jordan and Lebanon, we also conducted six focus-group discussions with six to nine Syrian refugees each: segregated groups of men and women in two different age categories (ages 18–35 and 36–65). All focus-group participants resided in or near Amman and Beirut and ranged widely in their education levels. Among the women, some were heads of households and others were not. Each focus group was organized by a different NGO, with RAND providing criteria for selection of participants. Focus groups were held on site at NGO facilities in most cases. In one case, a focus group was held at a hotel selected by the NGO. To ameliorate bias in discussions, NGO officials were not present during the discussions, and our questions did not address the performance of any particular NGO, but rather focused on general public-service issues. Among the focus-group participants, the fact that they were already in contact with an NGO (and therefore receiving some sort of NGO service) may be a source of bias; however, we aimed to address this by asking both about their personal experiences and the experiences of other refugees that they know. Focus-group discussions addressed how refugees settled and met basic needs upon arrival, how they sustain access to social services and their needs over time, challenges particular to each gender, and access to information.

RAND's human subjects protection committee and its policies guided our interview and focus group processes. As part of the interview process, we told interviewees that, while we would aggregate their views, we would not identify individuals. We do, when feasible, identify majority and minority views and frequently note the kinds of stakeholders with particular views (e.g., donor representatives, UN agency officials, NGO leadership, government officials, or international experts).

This report is organized into four chapters and two appendixes. Chapter Two describes tensions between humanitarian, resilience, and development aid and coordination models, and proposes a new framework for bridging them. Chapter Three provides an overview of how aid for the refugee crisis is coordinated in Jordan and Lebanon, focusing on participants' roles, coordination structures and strategies, budgets and money flows, and information. Chapter Four concludes the report with recommendations. Appendix A describes coordination of services in the six sectors analyzed in this report in Jordan and Lebanon, with particular analysis of how they relate to the framework developed in Chapter Two. Finally, Appendix B details our interview and focus-group protocols.

CHAPTER TWO

Evolving Models of Urban Refugee Responses

The international assistance community is reassessing approaches to refugee assistance in humanitarian emergencies. This reassessment has two important components. The first is recognition that response models that assume that most refugees live in camps are no longer viable. Instead, it is necessary to create mechanisms and procedures that enable host countries to respond to the needs of refugees living among the urban and rural populations. The second is the related recognition that, because refugees are interspersed with local communities and because local authorities are critical components of any response, emergency humanitarian responses for refugees must be linked to host-country development plans.

Effective new approaches have been slow to develop. This chapter discusses the efforts made to date to adapt new response models, emphasizing the implications for coordination and proposing an alternative framework for planning and evaluating coordination of the refugee crisis in Jordan and Lebanon (and potentially in other urban refugee crises). This framework will serve as a basis for analysis in the following chapters.

From Camps to Urban Areas

Until 2009, the primary focus of UNHCR was provision of services to refugees in camps. The reality of displacement crises today is that at least half of all refugees settle in non-camp areas, including cities, villages, informal tented settlements, and shantytowns

(UNHCR, 2015c). They do so for many reasons. Refugees perceive that urban and other non-camp areas can offer freedom of movement, employment opportunities, and better provision of services such as education and health care. Refugees who settle in urban and other non-camp areas have better long-term outcomes in terms of self-sufficiency than refugees in camps (UNHCR, 2015c). Furthermore, the camp approach is inherently short term by intention: It is meant to provide a temporary solution to displacement. Yet, many refugee crises are long term. In 2014, 45 percent of the world's refugees were in a protracted situation (defined as lasting longer than five years), and the average duration of a protracted refugee situation is 25 years (UNHCR, 2015c)—meaning large numbers of refugees are displaced for one or more generations. As a result, forcing the displaced into restricted camps that depend on international assistance is not humane to the refugees or financially sustainable to donors. Indeed, one refugee in Jordan interviewed for this report described camps as "not fit for humans."

Given the decreasing reliance on camps for refugees, UNHCR has issued guidance promoting integration of refugees into the urban fabric of host countries (UNHCR, 2009). In 2011, UNHCR published additional guidance on refugees in urban areas, intended to help implement the new refugee policy in education, health, and employment (UNHCR, 2011a; UNHCR, 2011b; UNHCR, 2011c).

In 2012, UNHCR assessed how well the new policy had been implemented, noting that "refugees' increasing presence in urban areas signifies a seismic shift in the way UNHCR operates, and it presents both challenges and opportunities" (Morand et al., 2013). It concluded that there are "very real gaps, challenges, and constraints in working with urban refugees." In another review, UNHCR Interagency Standing Working Group concluded "donors have yet to develop strategies for designating funds for humanitarian operations in urban areas" (Zetter and Deikun, 2010). These assessments cited two main challenges.

First, many services to refugees rely less on aid agencies (such as the UN and NGOs) and more on line ministries, municipal authorities, the private sector, police, civil society actors, and community groups.

Refugees attend local public schools, seek medical care in public clinics and hospitals, rent housing from the housing market, make use of water and sanitation systems, and find jobs with local businesses. This is a different situation than in refugee camps, where the primary service providers are international humanitarian agencies, not established governments, civic associations, and the private sector. This means that more types of actors need to work together effectively than in a camp. The UNHCR assessments pointed to the need for changes in coordination in urban areas (and research about how to do so), and engagement with this wider range of actors.

Second, refugees adapt best when they can become self-reliant, gain employment, meet many of their own needs, contribute to their communities, and take care of themselves and their families (Morand et al., 2013; UNHCR, 2009; UNHCR, 2011c; Zetter and Deikun, 2010). In principle, this should be easier to accomplish in integrated, non-camp settings than in segregated camps. However, there is a significant lack of knowledge about how best to facilitate such self-reliance among urban refugees. Urban refugees face a host of additional or exacerbated challenges that include: government policies restricting employment or access to services; competition with host-country urban poor for services and employment; inadequate and overcrowded shelters; harassment and discrimination; vulnerability to sexual and gender-based violence; and food insecurity (Feinstein International Center, 2012; Landau, 2008; UNHCR, undated[a]; UNHCR, 2009; UNHCR, 2011c; "The Urban Challenge for Refugees," 2013; Zetter and Deikun, 2010).

Thus, when the Syrian refugee crisis began in 2011, despite the recognition of the changes in UNHCR's 2009 guidance about managing refugee crises, much of the experience that the humanitarian community brought to the Syrian crisis was from camps in other refugee crises. Much of that experience was also with crises with refugees from poor countries or failed states to other poor countries or failed states. For example, in 2010, the biggest refugee populations were from Afghanistan, the Democratic Republic of the Congo, Iraq, Myanmar, and Somalia (UNHCR, 2011d). By contrast, Syria was a middle-income country, and the three main hosts of the Syrian refugees

(Turkey, Lebanon, and Jordan) are also middle-income countries, with thriving cities and robust public and private sectors.

While the international humanitarian community recognized the need for new approaches, the Syrian refugee crisis offered stark evidence that the world might need to move more quickly on this issue (Crisp et al., 2013). Multiple interviewees for this report also pointed to the disconnect between previous approaches and the current urban refugee crisis. One claimed, "The humanitarian community is not equipped to respond to an urban crisis." Another explained, "In middle-income countries, it is expensive when you take what you do in south Sudan and try to do it here." Yet another noted, "The old refugee model of coming in with a flood of resources and then leaving is not relevant here."

Most importantly, for this report, we emphasize that non-camp settings require far broader cooperation than is needed in camps. More organizations are involved with refugee assistance, and absent effective mechanisms to ensure that their work is complementary, may inadvertently be ineffective or waste resources while trying to help refugees.

From Humanitarianism and Development to Resilience—or Not

Many of our interviewees (particularly those representing the international aid community) posited what appeared to be two disconnected assistance models: humanitarian responses employed temporarily for emergencies and development interventions for economic growth and improvement of public services. Many see this "relief-development tension" as the fundamental problem in crises such as this one, which combine an emergency humanitarian response with longer-term development efforts (Buchanan-Smith and Maxwell, 1994).

Multiple stakeholders, including government representatives, with whom we spoke in Lebanon and Jordan, argued that "humanitarian" responses had not achieved desired results in meeting the short- and longer-term needs of the refugees, and national development plans had yet to integrate the needs of the refugees and the host communities affected by the refugees. The refugee crisis had evolved to engulf the countries as a whole, as well as their development agendas, straining their resources and degrading infrastructure. Those we spoke with characterized the situation as a "combustible package" that is "morphing from a humanitarian crisis to a development crisis." Despite the evidently protracted nature of the situation, assistance efforts focus primarily on short-term plans, while national development goals are sidelined. Indeed, one complained, "At the local level, humanitarian work and development work do not touch."

Given the assumption that a gap needed to be bridged between humanitarian and development responses, both the international community and local authorities began to make efforts to do so.

With growing recognition that the refugee crisis was becoming protracted, the UN-sponsored 2015 Refugee Response and Resilience Plan (3RP) for the Syrian refugee crisis attempted to combine a refugee humanitarian response with host-country development considerations. Using the term "resilience" to blend the two approaches, this was the first time that the UN had been involved in combining the two, calling it a "paradigm shift" (3RP, 2015a). (In Lebanon, the term "stabilization" is used instead of resilience.) The 3RP purports to be nationally led by the host countries, while involving inputs from more than 200 national and international partners. Resilience was meant to be the crossroad between the humanitarian response and development in the face of a prolonged crisis. In coordination with the 3RP, Jordan also developed its national version, the 2015 Jordan Response Plan (JRP) (MOPIC, 2015a, and UNOCHA, 2014), and Lebanon developed the 2015 Lebanon Crisis Response Plan (LCRP) (UNOCHA, 2014).

While recognizing the need for a new model as an important step, most of those we spoke with, across the range of roles, noted that there is no consensus on what "resilience" means, with one calling it a "buzz word" and another saying that people are still "struggling with the concept." One UN official interviewed noted that resilience "doesn't have a clear definition or mean much by anyone's standards." Several of those we spoke with argued that current models are not working and that the international community should fundamentally rethink the aid architecture and coordination of the crisis. Meanwhile, local government officials often expressed views that the international community's efforts are misaligned with government priorities and sovereignty. Conversely, many international humanitarian officials complained that governments were failing to take on leadership and were unable to manage coordination, both because of political gridlock and lack of capacity.

All this raises the possibility that the problem, particularly in coordination, may not be one of different models, but dueling perspectives of what needs to be done. Most of the humanitarian community sees its primary duty as assisting refugees. It is uncomfortable with programs focused on host communities, even if they also benefit refugees. Some of those we spoke with expressed concern that responses focused on long-term national capacity would fail to address the immediate emergency needs of the refugees. Conversely, host governments and development actors prefer to spend their scarce resources on supporting communities, municipalities, and the state. Some told us that it would not be productive to divide people who live among one another by nationality. Coordination challenges, then, were not so much a result of ineffective communication and information sharing as they were products of competing views of what is important. We posit that, to overcome those challenges, it may be helpful to identify who holds which views and adjust expectations so that actors can focus on their own priorities, while working to ensure that all needs are met. The next section proposes a mechanism for doing this.

A Framework for Coordination of the Crisis

Generalizing the problem as one of competing humanitarian and development approaches masks the specific disagreements and misalignments at stake, precluding addressing each in turn. We propose a framework that identifies tensions within five different (if somewhat overlapping) lenses to view the specific issues at stake, which we call "approach areas," identified through analysis of our interview notes and the literature review. These lenses or approach areas are: time frame (short- versus medium-term planning and activities), the nature of services for the refugees (integrated with those of the host community or a parallel set run by the international community), leadership of coordination (international versus local), destination of funding (to international organizations versus national organizations), and the focus of interventions (on refugees versus on the host communities that have absorbed refugees). Other dichotomies are possible. We identify these as the most relevant in the context of refugee response in Jordan and Lebanon. Figure 2.1 illustrates these approach areas. They align somewhat with the models discussed (i.e., the approaches in the left column are often, but not always, correlated with one another, as are the approaches in the right column). However, the approach areas also provide a means to break the models down into component parts and understand how these factors actually influence coordination and response. This focus on specifics makes it possible to understand implications for coordination. Stakeholders have preferences regarding many, but often not all, of these, and those preferences will determine how they work together—or fail to.

In each case, there are choices to be made between two broad approaches. How each of these approach areas is viewed by each stakeholder for any given issue (e.g., health care, education) has significant implications for how services are coordinated: who is in charge, how roles are defined, how actors relate to one another, how planning is conducted, skills that are needed, demands on funders, funding sources, assumptions, priorities, relief provision, and structures.

Figure 2.1
A Framework of Approach Areas for Coordination of the Refugee Crisis

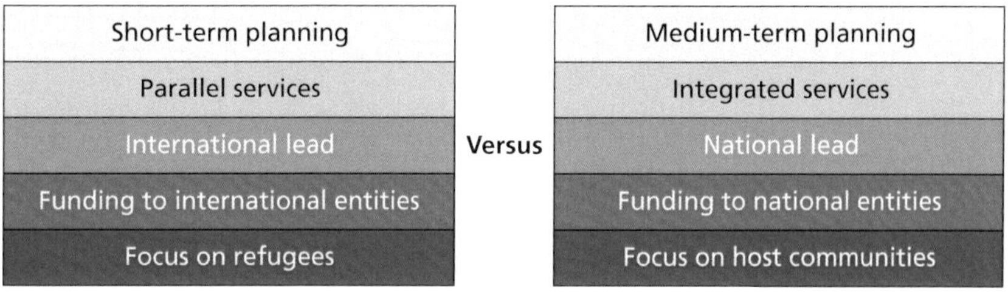

RAND *RR1485-2.1*

We do not believe that there is a single right answer to any of these approach areas, regardless of the circumstance. Indeed, often action is needed at both ends of the spectrum, and different stakeholders will feel more comfortable acting in different parts of that space. Instead of a rigid model, we propose the approach areas as a checklist to consider when planning and evaluating coordination of various sectors of the response to refugee crises. For each approach area, coordination planners should consider where stakeholders stand. This can enable more-effective acceptance of perspectives as well as allocations of roles of the various stakeholders, as appropriate in each individual case. We anticipate that this will differ by sector. For example, in education in Lebanon, the Ministry of Education and Higher Education is taking additional leadership of refugee education (a national lead), but lacks the capacity to expand school spaces, instead relying on international actors (funding to international entities). Below we discuss each approach area in turn and, in the Appendix A, we lay out how these approach areas have been addressed in the six sectors analyzed: legal; employment; shelter; water, sanitation, and hygiene (WASH); health care; and education.

Short- Versus Medium-Term Planning

The time-frame dichotomy is one of the biggest perceived differences between humanitarian and development models. It addresses whether planning is for the short- or long-term and whether it focuses on emergency or investment needs. One would expect an emergency response to involve life-saving assistance to meet urgent short-term needs. Investment, by contrast, promotes longer-term sustainability, improvements, or growth. However, the two do not match perfectly to development and humanitarian models. Many humanitarian crises are long term, and many activities involved, such as education and health care, have a sustainability component. Similarly, aspects of development approaches, such as improving infrastructure, also address immediate needs.

Refugee crises are rarely either/or situations. Ideally, short-term responses will support (or at least not undermine) sustainability, and sustainability efforts will provide for at least some immediate needs.

However, the planning of the response must take into account the important question of whether the crisis itself is a lasting one.

In the Syrian refugee crisis, and likely in many displacement crises, neither the scale nor the time frame could have been predicted. According to many we interviewed, both the international community and the host countries substantially underestimated the numbers of refugees and the duration of the crisis. As numbers grew and it became clear that the war would continue, host governments faced political constraints that precluded planning for a long-term situation. This remains the case, although privately, government officials in both Jordan and Lebanon acknowledged that the Syrians will be in their countries for a number of years. As one official noted, a long-term time frame was "too much to swallow for the host country, donors, and UNHCR." Preferring "stabilization," the government of Lebanon even found the word "resilience" problematic, fearing it implied a long-term crisis.

Both initial uncertainty about time frame and political limitations made planning difficult. While short-term planning made sense early, when all (erroneously) expected that the crisis would end quickly, it was soon clear that it would not be sufficient. One international expert told us, "The gap is partially mindset—we respond to emergencies as if they are short-term rather than recognizing that the majority of them aren't, which requires starting in a different place."

The approach to time frames has implications for coordination. Short-term planning is based on the view that refugees need only near-term help prior to their return to their home countries. This means six-to-12-month funding cycles with temporary programs; until the end of 2014, each funding appeal for the Syrian refugee crisis was based on six-month plans. The 2015 3RP has a two-year time frame, which is still doubtless shorter than the crisis will endure. These "humanitarian band aids" (as one interlocutor put it) crowd out investments that may be needed to meet longer-term needs, such as expanding and sustaining refugees' access to public services, including the construction of additional schools, hospitals, or sanitation infrastructure. Implementing NGOs in particular noted how difficult sustaining programs and staffs could be when budgets from donors and permissions from governments are short term. Governments cannot invest in expansion of public services when funding is stopgap. Interviewees in Jordan believed that the emergency response hampered the longer-term vision to the whole response. One NGO official in Jordan noted, "We wasted four years trying to respond to immediate needs. Now funds are getting shorter."

Short-term approaches are appropriate for urgent, short-lived needs. They become a problem when a crisis becomes protracted. One way this is manifested is in the choice of parallel or integrated services.

Parallel Versus Integrated Services

Parallel services are new services developed and implemented by UN agencies and NGOs with donor funding, parallel to those provided to local citizens by their own government. These may be short or long term, but they are different from national or local public services already in place. Refugee camps, for example, are a pure parallel-service model, wherein the international community provides for the full range of refugee needs (such as shelter, schools, and clinics).

Integrated services, by contrast, are those that the host country provides to refugees as it provides them to their citizens, sometimes with technical, financial, or implementation support from donors, UN agencies, or NGOs (e.g., allowing refugees access to public schools and hospitals).

Historically, humanitarian aid often relies on parallel-service provision because it is often carried out where local governments cannot or will not provide assistance or provide it quickly enough. In the immediate wake of natural disaster or conflict, this can be critical. But because it "almost always bypasses central state institutions, and does little to build state capacity beyond the local level" (Organization for Economic Coordination and Development [OECD], 2012), stakeholders may conclude that relief aid is not helping or is exacerbating the situation (Harvey and Lind, 2005).

While parallel services are not explicitly designed to broaden local capacity, they can nonetheless develop local infrastructure and may be sustainable. For example, new schools and hospitals for the refugee community might be given to local governments for future operations.

If they are not, they can only be sustained with a long-term commitment of donor funding, as was the case with UN Relief and Works Agency for Palestine Refugees in the Near East (UNRWA) schools for Palestinian refugees throughout the Middle East. Since 1967, UNRWA has run the largest nongovernmental school system in the Middle East with donor funding, educating 500,000 Palestinian children in Lebanon, Jordan, Syria, the West Bank and Gaza (UNRWA, undated). This means that, for half a century, these communities have been educated in a system segregated from that offered to the citizens of the countries where they live.

A central argument of this report is that the model of heavy reliance on long-term parallel services is failing, a sentiment widely expressed (although described in different ways) by multiple interviewees from UN agencies, governments, NGOs both in Jordan and Lebanon, and at agency headquarters. The parallel-service model contributes to segregation of society, is expensive, undermines capacity of national governments, and fosters dependency on international actors. In Jordan and Lebanon, there is fear of repeating the UNRWA experience. Some interviewed argued that refugee assistance should have worked more consistently by expanding existing public services in Jordan and Lebanon from the start. "The international community is trying to substitute for the government with short-term initiatives," noted one UN official at headquarters. Another official stated:

> They have social services to a relatively good standard. In this crisis, we have created a parallel system rather than getting behind those systems. This was a case where there were systems in place, flawed but capable, and we didn't get in to support them, but set up a very costly parallel system, not accountable to the government.

Another multilateral official in Lebanon said, "The government should feel its capacity built. Otherwise, we move from capacity building to capacity substitution. Then you see other agencies delivering services, not always more efficiently, not leaving anything behind."[1]

Supporting integrated services presents substantial challenges, particularly early in a crisis, and transitioning from parallel to integrated services later poses similar issues. Government bureaucracies can make it difficult to do things fast, which may mean that assistance does not reach those who need it. Governments may have difficulty deciding what approaches to approve. The UNHCR Inter-Agency Standing Working Group also concluded:

> Perhaps the biggest challenge for humanitarian actors—and also a major opportunity—is to develop ways of working with the existing institutional framework of municipal and civil society organizations which exists in most towns and cities in the developing world" (Zetter and Deikun, 2010).

Interviewees among UN agencies and NGOs explained that they created parallel systems because it was easier and faster than trying to work through the government or local entities.

But whether near- or long-term assistance is at issue, providing for refugees settled among host communities makes parallel-assistance approaches difficult. While it is possible to set up separate clinics, schools, and other facilities to support refugees only, the diffusion of displaced populations within the host community strengthens the argument for working through existing institutions and infrastructure. Then, as one interviewee pointed out, the question becomes one of facilitating access to existing services, supporting existing services, and creating referral pathways to those services, not creating new services. For the international community to support access, it should work with the range of stakeholders involved rather than simply funding UN agencies and NGOs to create new programs or infrastructure. And the aid community as a whole, including government actors as

---

[1] It is worth noting that those we spoke with also represent their agencies and organizations. On points such as this, where there are—as will be shown in the rest of this report—clear positions held by different organizations, many reported views aligned with organizational interests.

well as international organizations, should make decisions based on recognition of what services refugees can access in existing systems and what specialized services should be added.

The 3RP strongly favors integrated over parallel services:

> Reinforcing national capacities is an overarching priority to make the collective response more cost-effective and sustainable over the long run, and to reduce the degree to which parallel service delivery systems are established (3RP, 2015b).

Programs or budgets do not always reflect these priorities, as we discuss in the next section.

Internationally Versus Nationally Lead

The dichotomy of whether leadership of coordination is from the international community or the host government aligns in some ways with others discussed above. One can envision a choice between near-term, parallel structures supported by international actors and long-term, integrated structures built by the host government. The reality, however, is more complicated, demonstrating the need to differentiate between these areas. Even if the response is long term and integrated, international organizations may take the lead, given their greater capacity, or government actors may take the lead on coordinating parallel services when their own services are not sufficient.

Generally speaking, an international lead means a UN lead. For a refugee situation, UNHCR has the lead on coordination with the local government, donors, other UN agencies, and NGOs. A national lead means that the government determines priorities and integrates international organizations, NGOs, and others into its planning.

UN leadership may be most needed early in a crisis, when fast responses with special approaches are needed (such as in establishing parallel-service structures, mobilizing funding from donors, or hiring implementing NGOs) and governments are not capable of coordinating them. Politics in Lebanon make rapid decisionmaking a challenge, which left little choice but a strong international lead role early on.

As time passes, sovereign states seek to manage a crisis on their soil, even as they may continue to rely on foreign assistance. This is particularly true when refugees are not segregated into camps. UN and NGO interviewees in both countries acknowledged that they have not done well in including Lebanese and Jordanian institutions to build their capacity to take over. There were repeated comments from international experts that the response did not engage with governments soon enough, sacrificing sustainability for speed.

Funding to International Entities Versus Funding to National Entities

The questions of who leads, and whether services are parallel or integrated, are inextricably tied to the question of who manages the money contributed by external donors. Should it be the government, or should it be UN agencies and NGOs? Does this vary by assistance type and specific situation? The answer to the last question is almost certainly yes, but donor aid money is nearly always channeled through UN agencies and NGOs. Determining a better path forward is still difficult. Best use of funds and cost effectiveness are among the determinants of the right choices in this area (Buchanan-Smith and Maxwell, 1994).

In the Syrian refugee crisis, the 3RP principles indicate that local capacity should be a priority. Funding has generally gone first to international organizations, from which it then flows to local organizations and the refugees themselves. As noted earlier, $4.5 billion of the $5.5 billion requested in the 2015 3RP was allocated to UN agencies and international NGOs, with $1 billion requested for governments (3RP, 2015a). With that proportion of requested funding for the international aid community, rather than to host governments and civil societies, funding is not available to help build longer-term capacity of the host countries to manage future services. While the UN agencies and international NGOs hire host-country citizens in addition to their international staff, it appears that refugee-response funding is going primarily toward institutions of the international aid community.

Should funding go to whoever is overseeing the relevant assistance? Should efforts to support national capacity and service provision be aligned with funding that goes through national structures, whether government or NGO? A review of the 3RP budgets shows that, even when governments have expanded access to public services (for example, with Jordan opening public education and health care systems to refugees and Lebanon opening its education system), a disproportionate amount of funding requested is for UN agencies or NGOs. Even some in the international-assistance community question this direction of funding: One interviewee noted, "This needs more than UN agencies handling money. The government needs to get in the driver's seat.

There are a number of challenges inherent in channeling donor funds into direct budget support to governments. In some cases, donor funding is mandated toward international agencies (e.g., PRM's budget is congressionally mandated to mainly fund the UN system and other international structures) or goes to international agencies out of habit. In other cases, there are concerns about budget support to the governments because of perceptions of weak accountability systems, views that governments lack the capacity to use the funding, or political constraints, such as that regarding U.S. support for Lebanon. Several donor-government representatives suggested to us, based on their evolving understanding of the situation, that these issues could be resolved. A resolution, for instance, could be if donor assistance also helped governments to ensure that safeguards and policies are in place for financial management and procurement at a level acceptable to the international community.

Focus on Refugees Versus on Host Communities

Another difference is the focus of assistance, whether the assistance is targeted only at the refugees or whether it is targeted toward helping host communities, including refugees. According to interviewees, these differences are evident in competing approaches of UNHCR, the governments, and others. UNHCR's approach, in line with its mandate, has been to direct its resources in support of refugees. Others have argued that supporting host communities to expand their provision of education, health, or sanitation is a more sustainable and effective way to assist refugees; it also alleviates some of the political problems that might otherwise accompany refugee assistance. Both the governments of Jordan and Lebanon mandated that proportions of the humanitarian response target their own citizens to alleviate the impact of the refugees and lessen resentment of citizens seeing services they lack directed toward refugees. In the 3RP budgets, many indicators focus on the number of Syrians served by a particular program, and how that number compares with the number of host-country citizens served. Such a benchmark may be difficult to measure and misleading because it fails to capture how host communities can expand their capacity to provide for their citizens and the refugees. It is also a short-term assessment rather than a measure of how national systems have been strengthened, improved, or expanded; instead it measures how many citizens can be served with the parallel services provided by NGOs.

Refugees need specific services (e.g., food assistance, legal protection, treatment for posttraumatic stress disorder) more so than members of the host community. It is appropriate to fund and support such services, although it is worth determining whether it can be done in a way that assures access to host-community members who also need such services.

Summary

The international assistance community is at a conceptual crossroads. It is moving from providing for refugees in camps to helping host-country urban areas absorb refugees. The international assistance community is working through ways to combine humanitarian assistance with development planning. Both of these issues have implications for coordination. While the assistance community recognizes that old approaches are not working, we assess that it has been inefficient in developing new approaches by focusing too much on a trade-off between "humanitarian" responses and "development" responses, rather than on the fundamental issues underlying these models. We propose a new framework that unpacks the perceived differences between the two response models into five approach areas. The new framework can be used to assess stakeholder priorities and inform both planning and evaluation of refugee-response coordination of services across sectors.

CHAPTER THREE

An Overview of Coordination in Jordan and Lebanon

An internationally led refugee response helped meet the needs of many refugees early in the crisis, no doubt saving lives. To do this, it relied on coordination mechanisms that had been used in other refugee responses. In Jordan and Lebanon, the response involved establishment of an expensive and time-consuming coordination structure. As the crisis continued, the response has increasingly been characterized by tensions among the UN agencies, between the governments and the international assistance community, and between international and local NGOs. Moreover, the approach has been blamed for marginalizing the refugees themselves, and many question how effectively donor money is being spent. Meanwhile, many public services in Jordan and Lebanon are now deeply overburdened, and aid money for parallel services provided by the international community is insufficient to meet needs. These issues have led to reconsideration of the coordination model in place and the roles and responsibilities of the major stakeholders. This chapter discusses coordination elements of the refugee response in Jordan and Lebanon in four contexts: who is involved, coordination structures, budgeting and money flows, and information.[1]

---

[1] The list of elements of coordination is derived from analysis of issues that interviewees raised as important in the coordination of the refugee response in Jordan and Lebanon, as well as of elements of coordination as described by UN agencies. Various UN agencies describe coordination in different ways. For example, UNICEF uses a framework of structures, functions, implementing coordination mechanisms, and skills (see UNICEF, 2010).

Who Is Involved

A wide range of organizations and groups play roles in the refugee crises in Jordan and Lebanon, creating a complicated web of coordination roles and responsibilities. Among them are governments, UN agencies, donors, NGOs, the private sector, the refugees themselves, and host communities. Each of these parties brings unique value to the response, as well as their own specific limitations. They also have different priorities, which has made it difficult to agree on goals and strategies for coordinating services. Below, we describe the current roles, priorities, values added, and limitations of the stakeholders, and then compare how their goals and priorities differ on the five approach areas of the coordination framework presented in Chapter Two.

Governments

In Jordan and Lebanon, roles in refugee-response coordination are played by multiple government entities: national political leadership, ministries, and municipalities.

Political leadership sets tone and policy and manages bilateral relations with donors. The governments of Jordan and Lebanon generously opened their borders to the refugees and offered them public services. At the same time, they also continue to express concern about maintaining security within their borders, not worsening their own high unemployment rates through an influx of Syrian labor, not further straining public services for their own citizens, harnessing humanitarian funding to benefit their development and goals, and ensuring that the Syrians eventually return home. Conflicting goals in different parts of government can lead to stalled decisionmaking. While this problem exists in both countries, it is particularly acute in Lebanon.

Neither the governments of Jordan nor Lebanon publicly acknowledge the potential medium-term nature of the refugee crisis. Officials in both countries have, from the start, feared that the long-term effects of this refugee situation would permanently change their countries'

UNOCHA considers coordination, policy, advocacy, information management, and financing (UNOCHA, undated[b]).

demographics, as the 1948 and 1967 waves of Palestinian refugees had done. Many of the Palestinian refugees, along with their descendants, remain in Jordan and Lebanon today.

Ministries manage public services at the national level. Jordan's Ministry of Planning and International Coordination (MOPIC) and Lebanon's Ministry of Social Affairs (MOSA) have taken central roles in coordination across sectors within their own governments and with the international community. Over time, both MOPIC and MOSA have asserted additional control over coordination of the refugee responses by increasing management of planning processes (such as the development of the Jordan Response Plan [JRP] and LCRP) as well as instituting processes for government approval of NGO projects. Line ministries have developed creative ways to accommodate refugees with already-existing services, while seeking to maintain services for their own citizens (e.g., expanding capacity in schools by adding second school shifts for the Syrians). The line ministries coordinate directly with the specific UN agencies that address issues in their sectors. Ministries face several limitations in coordination: There are not enough capable staff who can take the roles of coordination with other ministries as well as with the international community; there are language barriers that hinder collaboration with international partners; there is a lack of data systems and access to technology (in particular, in Lebanon, where many ministry staff lack access to computers); and there are financial accountability systems that are insufficient for donor confidence in monitoring how funds are spent and services provided.

Municipalities are responsible for some local services, in particular, shelter, water, and sanitation. Their roles, capacities, and priorities can vary greatly, according to interviewees. There have been several pilot efforts to work with municipalities to prioritize local refugee-response needs. When Lebanon's Council for Reconstruction and Development worked with municipalities in Lebanon and the United States Agency for International Development (USAID) worked with municipalities in Jordan to determine priorities for the refugee response, the municipalities listed issues and solutions that international partners had not considered. These included improving public safety by installing streetlights and investing in waste management and water treatment to support the greater demand for these by a larger population. These pilot prioritization efforts at the municipal level have largely been ad hoc, and there are no clear plans to systematically expand them.

UN Agencies

Multiple UN agencies are involved in the refugee response. UNHCR has overall charge of coordination of the refugee response in both countries and manages camps in Jordan. Other UN agencies contribute in sectors for which they have expertise, including the UN Office of the Coordinator for Humanitarian Affairs (UNOCHA) for humanitarian responses, the UN Development Programme (UNDP) for development planning, UNICEF for education, the World Health Organization (WHO) for health, and WFP for food assistance. Additional UN agencies involved in refugee response include the UN Educational, Scientific and Cultural Organization (UNESCO); the International Organization for Migration (IOM); the UN Population Fund (UNFPA); the UN Human Settlements Programme (UN-Habitat); the UN Office for Project Services (UNOPS); the Food and Agriculture Organization of the UN (UNFAO); the International Committee of the Red Cross (ICRC); the International Federation of the Red Cross and Red Crescent Societies (IFRC); the International Labour Organization (ILO); UNRWA; the UN Office of the United Nations Special Coordinator for Lebanon (UNSCOL); and UN Women. (As one Lebanese government official wryly pointed out, Lebanon has 12 ministries, but 20 UN agencies present.)

The UN agencies play multiple roles. They manage coordination among international stakeholders and governments, mobilize funding from donors, contract with NGOs to implement programs, decide on the allocation of much of the aid channeled through them, lead budget development for the refugee response, introduce innovative data practices, provide technical support to line ministries, lead policy discussions, and engage international expertise to address problems.

Slaughter and Crisp (2009) argue that UNHCR, in particular, has "been transformed from a humanitarian organization to one that shares certain features of a state." This is because it has taken on responsibilities such as providing public services (e.g., access to shelter, food, water, health care, and education). They note that this came about because UNHCR was responsible for managing services in weak or fragile states, in which governments lacked capability, and leading states had not intervened to resolve conflicts. While recognizing the importance of UNHCR's particular role in protection, Slaughter and Crisp recommend greater support for the role of the state in refugee crises. They also recommend consolidation of the strategies, efforts, and budgets of the multiple UN agencies involved in refugee crises.

Critics described differing priorities, poor relations, competition, and lack of data sharing among UN agencies. Differing UN agency priorities stem from the fact that each tends to focus on its particular sector and mandate, which may lead to more attention for refugees or host communities at the expense of the other. For example, while UNHCR's mandate is only for refugees, other UN agencies had mandates for the needs of host communities in Jordan and Lebanon before the refugee crisis. These UN agencies are also in some competition, seeking funding and visibility for limited resources. For example, in Lebanon, UNHCR is charged with coordinating the refugee response, and UNOCHA with the humanitarian crisis. This creates a division of labor that causes confusion and competition, despite the fact that the refugee crisis and humanitarian crisis are one and the same.

Donors

The United States, the EU, and Gulf States have been the most active donors in this crisis to date. The United States has provided the largest amount of funding ($572 million in 2015), followed by the United Kingdom ($182 million), Kuwait ($166 million), Germany ($154 million), the EU ($154 million), Canada ($86 million), Japan ($85 million), and others (3RP, 2015c). The United States has provided more funding than the next three largest donors combined. Most of this funding is classified as humanitarian funding and is allocated on short-term cycles, typically one year at a time. Funders, however, differ in approach and priorities.

U.S. funding for the refugee response comes from PRM, which has a congressional mandate to channel most funding through multilateral organizations. This precludes most funding directly to host countries. Moreover, Congress forbids direct bilateral funding to Lebanon as long as Hezbollah is part of the government. At the same time, USAID provides development assistance to the governments; this is coordinated to a small extent with refugee funding. While the United States is the largest donor, it has not sought a leadership role in refugee-response policy. While U.S. embassies raise refugee issues bilaterally with the governments of Jordan and Lebanon, refugee-policy issues have taken lower priority than other issues in bilateral relations with these countries. Yet, multiple interviewees noted that the United States is the only donor large enough to have influence with the governments of Jordan and Lebanon. One representative of another donor government noted, "I don't know what PRM is funding. They make their decisions without consultation. The U.S. doesn't ask much. They just give money," implying a lack of consultation with other donors about coordinating policies. A leading NGO official in Lebanon argued that, "The U.S. is not using the leverage it should have. The U.S. is not present in coordination here."

The leading European donors are the United Kingdom Department for International Development (DFID), the EU Humanitarian Aid and Civil Protection, and German Federal Foreign Office Humanitarian Aid Division. Interviewees described that funding from these entities is also divided between humanitarian assistance and development, and agencies are struggling to create links to coordinate the different streams of funding, which are institutionally separated. The EU is focusing its efforts on health and protection, as well as strengthening institutional capacity of the government ministries. DFID is focusing on food and basic needs items, as well as health care.

The Gulf State countries are also significant, although largely unacknowledged, donors with important roles. As the third largest donor, Kuwait hosted the 2015 Third Pledging Conference in Kuwait City, in collaboration with UNOCHA. Gulf donors provide funding to the UN system, directly to governments (e.g., to Lebanon, which the United States and countries of the EU will not do), or to faith-based NGOs. For example, the Kuwait Fund provided funding to the government of Lebanon for emergency rooms in hospitals and for expansion of sanitation systems. A range of interviewees noted that the Gulf donors largely stay outside of the other coordination efforts, although there is some coordination between the Gulf countries and UNHCR on these issues. Yet, at the same time, multiple stakeholders noted widespread impressions that some Gulf funding is viewed as "dirty money," either intentionally funding family members of fighters in violent factions or lacking the accountability systems and logistics structures to channel their aid as planned. As one donor representative said, "The system is focused on traditional donors. It leaves a black hole in understanding what is being done by other actors." Several refugees in focus groups also observed that some Gulf aid is perceived as being used for "photo ops" and then somehow diverted, not reaching the refugees.

NGOs

There are several types of NGOs involved in the refugee response. Most relevant to our discussion are international, local, and faith-based (typically either international Christian organizations or local or regional Islamic) NGOs.

International NGOs are among the most important implementing partners that provide foreign-funded services to refugees. They are typically contracted and supervised by UN agencies, although donor-country agencies in some cases contract directly with NGOs, and some get private funding. International NGOs can mobilize needed international expertise, institutional capacity, and funding quickly in a crisis. They take on roles in service provision that the governments would have trouble performing, such as fast expansion of mental health services or data gathering among refugees. NGO presence is not sustainable in the long term without outside funding, as they leave when international funding ends. Some international officials observed a skill-set mismatch among NGOs operating in middle-income countries, as their experience was built managing programs in failed states: "NGOs prefer to not shift from service delivery to capacity building. They fear losing their role. Saying that you are running a clinic is more appealing than saying we are slowly building the government capacity." The international NGOs in both countries coordinate with one another through organized International NGO Forums.

Local NGOs also implement programs funded by international organizations, donors, governments, or private sources. Local NGOs have differing levels of capabilities and variable presence in coordination structures. While their programs can be less expensive than those of international NGOs, local NGOs may lack capacity in some cases. Several explained that they experienced difficulty receiving funding from donors and UN agencies, as language barriers and lack of proposal-writing experience serve as impediments to gaining larger roles.

Faith-based NGOs get their funding from some of the same sources that the international NGOs do (UN agencies, donor funding, etc.), as well as from private donations or state donors with religious goals. Faith-based NGOs also provide public services. Some of our interviewees viewed some of these NGOs very positively, as refugees often trust them. Several have a significant presence in coordination structures. At the same time, some of the local and regional organizations do not participate in coordination structures and have made little effort to integrate into the broader aid community (which, conversely, has also not reached out to them). These therefore remain "a world apart that is not integrated," as one interviewee described it. Many interviewees acknowledged their activities are not visible, creating concern about messaging and perceptions of sectarian support in some cases.

The Private Sector

The private sector has played an important role in the refugee response, although it has not participated much in formal policy coordination structures. Shelter and employment are largely a function of private-sector markets in urban areas, although government and UN policies and activities have significant impact, and NGOs often engage the private sector directly. The private sector provides rental housing, food, and other materials via markets, telecommunications, banking, and more. Companies and farms benefit by hiring Syrians in the informal market and from the refugees directly, as they are new consumers in shops. Both the labor markets in Jordan and Lebanon were already hiring Syrian labor before the crisis. In addition, health and education are highly privatized in Lebanon, with 70 percent of Lebanese children attending private schools and with more than 86 percent of hospital beds being privately owned (Aranki and Kalis, 2014).

Refugees

Rarely do refugees participate in the response, other than as recipients of aid. Most international and local stakeholders involve refugees as recipients, rather than as participants and decisionmakers (exceptions, for example, include international NGOs helping fund refugee volunteers to assist other refugees). Thus, while the Syrian refugees are the focus of coordination of the refugee response, they are not included in coordination structures. This means that decisionmaking roles of Syrian refugees about the services they receive is limited to what outreach the aid community chooses to undertake (e.g., occasional surveys and focus groups, as well as interactions with specific refugees). As a consequence, the refugees often lack a voice. Syrian refugees in both countries have made little effort to organize to improve their voice, no doubt in part because the demands of survival and subsistence leave little in the way of time or resources. Another factor limiting organization may be the diversity of the community. The divisions between various groups in Syria remain in place in Jordan and in Lebanon.

Our own focus groups with refugees revealed increasing desperation about access to services, in particular health care, and being able to obtain employment. In Jordan, refugees perceived that, in the past, education and health care were of better quality and more available; overall services and attitudes toward them were deteriorating. "Earlier in the crisis, people were more compassionate. Now there is less assistance, and it is harder for everyone," explained one man. In Lebanon, even more so than in Jordan, the pervasive sense of hopelessness among the refugee participants in our focus groups seemed worse, as many recounted trauma, injuries, untreated illnesses, children kept sequestered at home and not developing properly, children having to work on the street to prevent starvation, and people dying because they could not access health care. "There is no hope. The future of my children is lost," said one. "Because everything is overwhelming with the living conditions, we can only be pessimistic," said another. It is small wonder that some refugees are seeking to migrate to Europe, and many asked if we could help them leave.

Our focus groups also revealed that refugees do not understand what services are available and under what conditions, or why and how some receive aid and others do not. While UN officials and NGOs explained that decisions about allocation of scarce aid are based on vulnerability assessments, refugees often do not know this, and those that do perceive minor distinctions in vulnerability that make little sense. As a result, refugees we met, particularly in Lebanon, perceived aid as random, unfair, corrupt, unequal, insufficient, or unresponsive. Many had stories, their own or anecdotal, of needy people who did not get assistance, and others less needy who received plenty, leading them to think that "getting help depends on who you know." One said, "I am sure that Syrian refugees are getting a lot of assistance, but it is not getting to us." One NGO official acknowledged that this perception among refugees was not unfounded: "Why some get assistance and others do not is not well explained. Differences between those who got it and those who don't is small."

Some challenges are unique to girls and women, others to boys and men. Women take on new roles as heads of households when a man is missing, ill, or less able to get paid work, which is often the case among the refugees in both countries, although we heard more examples in Jordan. "Women are now men," explained one woman. Mobility is a challenge for women, restricting their ability to access information and services. Women may have difficulty finding work because they cannot leave their children alone. Men are more likely to be "caught working," (as they described it) and then arrested and sent back to Syria. The situation of refugees who identify as lesbian, gay bisexual, transgender, or intersex is particularly dire, with UN officials noting that they are more likely to have been tortured and that such refugees are given priority for asylum.

Host Communities

Like refugees, host communities are not officially part of coordination structures.[2] They receive services that their governments (at all levels) provide them, sometimes with international support. Unlike refugees, however, host communities in Jordan and Lebanon have some political power in that they can petition their local and national leaders for changes and organize politically, ensuring that they have more of a voice.

The host communities within which most refugees have settled in Jordan and Lebanon are poor and comparatively dependent on government services. Some members of those communities see the refugees as competition for scarce jobs and resources and are concerned that their presence increases the cost of housing, food, and other necessities. And even when host communities do not, as a whole, express these concerns, fears that they will do so may make politicians and government officials loath to support policies that would increase assistance to and freedom of work for refugees.

Comparison of Goals and Priorities

Stakeholders' goals, incentives, and priorities affect how they coordinate and manage the response. Our interviews strongly indicate that, as discussed in the previous chapter, what may at first appear to be coordination problems are actually driven by fundamental differences between stakeholders regarding what should be done, by whom, and for whom. These fundamental differences are about divergent views on the approach areas: over short- or long-term planning for the refugee crisis, whether refugee services should be managed by the international community or integrated with national efforts, whether leadership resides with international or national actors, who receives donor funding, and whether efforts aid only the refugees or include the host communities. These differences manifest in what seem to others to be

---

[2] It should be noted that host communities vary greatly. Some are located in urban areas, others are in rural; some are wealthier, while others are poorer; and some have substantial populations with kinship ties to the Syrian refugees, while others do not. These differences impact how communities respond to the refugees among them.

ineffectiveness, inefficiency, and sometimes even obstreperousness. As a result, the crisis has been characterized by failure to agree on goals within the governments, among the UN agencies, and between the international- and national-response communities. This is not a matter of coordination, but a matter of working at cross-purposes. "Each of us is thinking a different way and that affects the results," said a government official in Jordan.

Table 3.1 characterizes the key stakeholders by the approach areas, in line with the framework presented in Chapter Two. While there are variations among stakeholders, as well as exceptions, the table illus-

Table 3.1
Stakeholder Approaches to Five Issues

Stakeholder	Time Frame (Short- or Medium-Term)	Services (Parallel or Integrated)	Leadership (International or National)	Funding Recipients (International or National)	Focus (Refugees or Host Communities)
Governments	Short	Integrated	Both	National	Communities
Municipalities	Short	Both	Either	National	Communities
Private sector	Either	Integrated	Either	Either	Both
UNHCR	Short	Parallel	International	International	Refugees
Other UN agencies	Medium	Both	International	International	Both
Western donors	Short	Either	International	International	Refugees
Gulf donors	Short	Either	Either	Both	Refugees
International NGOs	Short	Parallel	International	International	Refugees
Local NGOs	Short	Parallel	Both	National	Both
Faith-based NGOs	Short	Parallel	Either	National	Both
Refugees	Short	Either	Either	Either	Both
Host communities	Medium	Either	Both	National	Communities

trates how stakeholders may base their actions on different preferences and assumptions about key issues. These disagreements are at the core of many of the challenges of response coordination.

We identify a number of patterns and insights from our overall findings and the comparisons in these tables:

- Not all stakeholders have strong views or preferences on all issues.
- Preferences of specific groups do not align perfectly with either the "development" or "humanitarian" models.
- Most stakeholders operate with short-term planning horizons for the refugee crisis.
- UNHCR and other UN agencies differ in their priorities, as UNHCR focuses solely on refugees and other UN agencies have broader mandates often similar to those of host-nation governments.
- UNHCR and international NGOs focused on refugee issues have similar sets of preferences, including with international leadership, parallel services, funding to international entities, and focus on the refugees.
- Western donors have similar profiles to UNHCR and international NGOs, except that Western donors do not have a strong preference between parallel and integrated services, as they are not the ones providing the services.
- There are divides between international actors (UN agencies and international NGOs) and host-country institutions on many issues.
- In some cases, governments also do not have clear preferences between parallel and integrated services, and their preferences may change over time. For example, in both countries, education ministries have insisted that formal certified education only be provided by their public schools, while supporting parallel catch-up and remedial programs offered by NGOs. At the same time, governments consistently do not want the refugees integrated into their labor markets.
- Refugees may prefer approaches that address the needs of host communities as well as their own. They seek access to common

services, including education, health, sanitation, and shelter, which will usually be more sustainable than internationally provided services. The exception may be services that are more needed by refugees than members of host communities, such as post-conflict trauma counseling.
- Host communities vary on their preference for parallel or integrated services, but they want to make sure that assistance to refugees neither comes at their expense nor is better than the support they receive.

Coordination Structures

The development of coordination structures followed similar patterns in Jordan and Lebanon, yet there are important differences. In the beginning of the crises, UNHCR took leadership of coordination, involving governments, other UN agencies, and NGOs. In 2014–2015, the governments of both Jordan and Lebanon stepped forward to exert more influence and control over coordination, demanding more consideration for addressing host community needs alongside refugee needs.

In Jordan, UNHCR-led coordination is based on the cluster system, the model typically used by UN agencies in displacement crises. The cluster system is an off-the-shelf toolkit of common practices (Humanitarian Response, undated; UNOCHA, undated[a]) for organizing UN officials and NGOs to provide services in various public sectors. UNHCR, other UN agencies, and NGOs took roles as leaders of sectors that included education, food security, health, protection, shelter, WASH, and more (UNHCR, 2015b). In no sector was the government listed as a sector lead. While government of Jordan representatives were formally invited to all meetings, multiple interviewees told us that government officials rarely attended for reasons that included language barriers, overburdened government staff, and differences in working culture between government officials and the humanitarian community. In 2014–2015, the government of Jordan introduced its own coordination structure through JRP. JRP did not replace UNHCR's sector-coordination system, but rather introduced an additional coordination structure with task forces as well as a secretariat. In addition to both of these superstructures, the coordination effort in Jordan includes various working groups and forums, such as the International NGO Forum.

UNHCR also created a coordination structure in the early years of the Lebanon response. This, however, did not follow the cluster-system framework. Instead, UNHCR led each of nine sectors (in contrast with Jordan, in which UNHCR, other UN agencies, and NGOs took various sector leadership roles). Several in the international community were upset by this choice, having familiarity with and training in the cluster system. They found UNHCR's decision to lead all sectors problematic. Staff from other UN agencies, particularly, felt that agencies specializing in certain sectors should have sector leadership. Those we spoke with described tensions among UN agencies that stem from unclear roles; turf battles between UNHCR and other UN agencies; lack of information sharing; bloated staff; and criticisms that UNHCR had built a system with inherent conflicts of interest because it was managing the money, choosing implementing partners, and implementing programs. There were particular tensions between UNHCR and UNOCHA, which felt it should have more leadership of the refugee response because of its mandate for humanitarian protection.

In the initial years of the crisis in Lebanon, the government preferred that the UN system manage the response. It was therefore not active in coordination structures. After several years, however, as in Jordan, the government of Lebanon stepped forward to take a stronger role. It created LCRP, a two-year plan and funding appeal for 2015–2017 (UNOCHA, 2014). Similar to JRP, LCRP is a strategic document with a set of estimated costs for the plan that emphasizes "stabilization" or investment for host communities as well as refugees. Like JRP, introduction of LCRP changed the coordination architecture. The government of Lebanon and UNDP took more active roles. UNDP stepped in as cochair with UNHCR of all nine sectors. UNHCR retained leadership of areas directly relevant to refugee support, while UNDP took the lead on "stabilization." To coordinate intra-UN positions, UN agencies in Lebanon established the "quartet" with the leadership of four UN agencies (UNHCR, UNDP, UNOCHA, and the UN Regional Coordinator's Office) working together in collaboration. Lebanon's MOSA took the lead on the overarching approaches, and the Ministry of Education and Higher Education (MEHE) and the Ministry of Health took over coordination leadership in their sectors. Most stakeholders now agree that the government of Lebanon lacks the capacity to take over full leadership of coordination in all sectors. However, many of those we spoke with argued that recent changes had improved coordination.

Budgeting and Money Flows

While refugee needs are growing worldwide, with ever-greater numbers of people displaced by violence, the budget of UNHCR decreased 10 percent from 2014 to 2015 (Grant, 2015). Also, as earlier noted, of the $5.5 billion that the UN-led 3RP appealed for to deal with the Syrian refugee crisis in 2015 (to be spread across Egypt, Iraq, Jordan, Lebanon, and Turkey), only $2.8 billion was funded by the end of 2015 (Financial Tracking Service, 2016). Given unrelenting refugee needs, tight budgets, and a crisis that will almost certainly not end in the near term, these trends are worrying. While a full budget analysis is outside the scope of this report, this section considers how budgets are coordinated, specifically: how budgets are developed and prioritized, where the money is sourced, how the funding is spent, how budget information is tracked, and the specific cost of coordination.

How budgets are developed and prioritized. The 2015 3RP budget appeal brought together the aid community and governments to tie together budget requirements for the refugee response and support for local needs. However, there are several challenges with the way that the budget request was developed. The 3RP budget was based on a coordinated consensus of the positions of governments and 200 international and national partners. They were not systematically based on needs assessments, options appraisals comparing cost effectiveness and efficiency, or prioritization efforts in the face of budget constraints. Several donors expressed cynicism about the budget, terming it "massive; they want everything," and a "wish list," that was "beyond the capacity of any donor." It could be argued that developing budgets for such a large operation based on the consensus of fund recipients could pose an inherent conflict of interest, as requests may reflect what the organizations want, rather than what is truly needed to meet refugee and community needs. Some items appear to be for parallel NGO-provided services that lack sustainability components (e.g., without plans for local authorities or NGOs to take on these roles in time) and others look like host-country development requests, independent of the refugee response. For example, JRP includes $64 million for university education, when there are few Syrians enrolled in Jordan's universities, and $30 million for job opportunities for Jordanians (The Jordan Response Platform for the Syria Crisis, 2015a).

Where the money comes from. Sources of funding for the refugee response include host governments, donors, and the refugees themselves. The $2.8 billion of the 2015 3RP that has actually been funded comes to approximately $660 per refugee per year, or less than $2 per day. Host governments primarily provide in-kind services. Meanwhile, refugees use their savings and any money that they are able to earn. For most, this is far from enough to meet the needs of daily life, which include food, shelter, electricity, sanitation, health care, education, and more. Increasingly, refugees and their children must either work illegally to supplement aid or risk starving. Yet, policies in Jordan and Lebanon are such that refugees are not officially allowed to work. Their labor is not considered a possible source of funding for the crisis. UN and NGO officials, as well as some donors interviewed, were concerned that raising this issue is a nonstarter with host governments, and that the only entity with the clout to address this issue is the United States.

Where the money goes. As discussed earlier, $1 billion of the UN-led funding appeal was allocated to the governments, and the remaining $4.5 billion to the UN system and NGOs; at the same time, there is also bilateral development assistance relevant to the refugee crisis that is not captured in these numbers. Out of the 2015 3RP request for Lebanon of $2.1 billion, only $169 million was slated for the government, with the rest to UN agencies and NGOs. For Lebanon, $1.4 billion was listed as the humanitarian component, with $0.7 billion as the stabilization component. In JRP, $0.9 billion was requested for the refugee component and $0.9 billion for the resilience component. The government of Jordan also requested $1 billion in support of direct operating costs, which the 3RP noted but did not endorse. (As of May 2015, the government of Jordan stated that none of its direct operating-cost request had been funded [MOPIC, 2015b].) Government agencies are frustrated that budgets flow to NGOs for provision of NGO services when the government is providing significant services at its own expense in education, health, and sanitation, and could expand services for refugees (e.g., in formal education) with additional donor funding. Budget-request allocations in the 3RP do not seem to reflect responsibility for service provision. At the same time, donors often prefer to route funding through UN agencies and NGOs rather than the governments for reasons that include mandates for humanitarian funding to be spent via UN agencies, concerns about accountability, and, in Lebanon's case, politics. While multi-donor trust funds have been tried, particularly in Lebanon, donors have viewed them as not fully dependable. Gulf donors, however, have no qualms about direct-aid provision to the governments. Therefore, Western money and Gulf money flow through different channels.

How budget information is tracked. Accounting is complicated because of the multiple types of funding streams (humanitarian, development, bilateral, multilateral) from numerous entities (donors from different countries, UN agencies, private groups) to other entities (UN agencies, NGOs, governments, contractors). In both countries, there are gaps in clearly accounting for funding sources, destinations, and amounts, due to the many donors, implementers, and recipients, and few centralized ways to aggregate their activities. However, the 2015 JRP effort placed a budgeting tracker online that covered some programming (The Jordan Response Platform for the Syria Crisis, 2015a). Accounting for the refugee response often does not take into account bilateral funding to governments or NGOs, funding from Gulf donors, national budgets that provide services, or development funding that is relevant to the humanitarian response. There is confusion about classifying and coordinating humanitarian- and development-aid streams. Humanitarian aid is often supported by different donor-country agencies than is development aid, although assistance may in fact be going to support similar organizations and programs. (In the United States, by way of example, PRM funds humanitarian efforts, while USAID funds development.) Even within governments, these funding efforts are often not well coordinated. As a result, donors are frustrated that governments cannot report how much money they have received from various sources, while governments are similarly unhappy that they lack a clear and complete picture of how aid funds from around the world are being spent in their countries.

The cost of coordination. The launch of a refugee response may not always be efficient, as a large number of organizations, individuals, and resources must be mobilized under uncertain conditions. As this refugee response passes into its fifth year, however, such expectations are no longer valid. Many of those we spoke with voiced concern that too much funding is spent on the coordination system itself, specifically on (1) staff time spent in coordination, (2) high overhead rates, and (3) budgets passing through multiple agencies.

First, as described earlier, the significant amounts of time that UN and NGO staff spend attending multiple parallel coordination meetings is a costly use of human resources (particularly true of well-compensated expatriate staff).

Second, many have questioned high overhead costs of UN agencies, exacerbated by the multiple pass-throughs (Cox, 2015; Hidalgo et al., 2015; "Where Does UK Aid to Syria Actually Go?" 2015). EU donors have been increasingly exasperated with the UN system's lack of financial transparency and high overhead costs for the Syrian refugee response. Palagashvili and Williamson (2014) found that UN agencies report higher administrative costs (66 percent) than bilateral or other multilateral donors (6 to 43 percent); have low amounts of aid dispersed per staff member (in comparison with other bilateral and multilateral donors); and saw an "extreme increase" of 30 percent in operating costs between 2004 and 2012, when other agencies were decreasing operating costs. Easterly and Pfutze (2008) found that "the data on aid agency spending are inexcusably poor," with the UN agencies "the worst" on transparency when compared with bilateral and multilateral agencies. The United States led the UN Transparency and Accountability Initiative to increase UN Member State oversight of UN agencies, "in light of the revelations in late 2006 and early 2007 of systemic abuses involving humanitarian and development activities in the UN's Funds and Programs," with the initiative leading to changes in financial-accountability practices for several UN agencies (US Mission to the United Nations, undated).

Third, costs were imposed when money passes through multiple entities before reaching service providers. The BBC report found that up to half of the budgets were spent on overhead for UN agencies and other middlemen. Figure 3.1 illustrates the multiple pathways that funding flows for the refugee response in Jordan and Lebanon. Funding flows from left to right, from donors onward through UN agencies, host governments, and implementers (NGOs, contractors, municipali-

Figure 3.1
Fiscal and Aid Flows

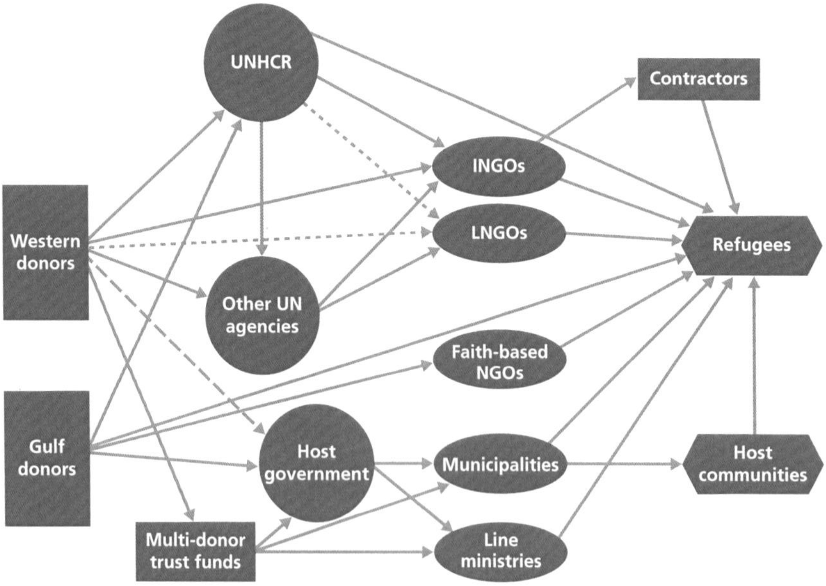

NOTE: The dotted lines represent weaker links than the solid lines.
INGOs = international NGOs; LNGOs = local NGOs.
RAND *RR1485-3.1*

ties, and line ministries) to the recipients (refugees and host communities). We note that this figure is difficult to read, as it illustrates the confusion of a complex and inefficient flow of funding. A more-efficient model would likely be easier to follow on paper, as well—and be far easier to audit. An example of one stream of funding in Figure 3.1 shows that funds go from donors to UNHCR. UNHCR may then provide funding to another UN agency, which funds an NGO. The NGO then contracts with other organizations. Each pass through each separate organization imposes overhead costs. Other funding streams go from donors to other UN agencies, then to NGOs and onward or from donors directly to NGOs. Many interviewees questioned this system. One asked, "Why all the middlemen? Each pass through an international organization takes at least 7 percent. Is this a good use of money?" One UN official described the budgets as "like leaking pipes," because of top-heavy coordination structures. "The humanitarian world became a business," lamented another.

Information

Multiple elements of information are important for coordination: information tools, information for the refugees, evaluations, and referrals.

Information tools. A number of innovative information practices have been developed or used in this refugee crisis in Jordan and Lebanon, including new uses of data and new information-sharing tools. UN programs use text messages to send information to refugees, as many refugees have cell phones. Use of iris scanning and biometrics during refugee registration is also used in cash-transfer programs. ActivityInfo (undated) is an online portal for aid workers that aims to track funded projects, help with referral of services, and analyze indicators. ActivityInfo was developed in Jordan and is now being used in Lebanon and Iraq. (Some noted that ActivityInfo improves transparency but depends on frequent inputs from stakeholders, which are not wholly reliable.) Furthermore, new tools help ensure that different organizations use the same criteria to determine refugees' eligibility for aid in each country: the Vulnerability Assessment Framework in

Jordan and the Vulnerability Assessment of Syrian Refugees in Lebanon (World Food Programme, 2013; UNHCR, 2014g). Development of these drew on expertise of multiple agencies in multiple sectors to develop indicators, surveys, and data as predictors of vulnerability. In Lebanon, UNOCHA developed maps that layer different data sets. The Refugee Assistance Information System is an information tool for aid workers that tracks which families were assisted in which sectors to reduce overlapping assistance (UNHCR, undated[b]). The 4W Atlas, an online information system, in Jordan aims to track "who does what where when" (MOPIC, 2015b). The UNHCR Information Portal provides documents across sectors and across countries (UNHCR, 2016c).

Information for the refugees. While information sharing among the aid community has been innovative, consistent information flow to the Syrians is insufficient. In focus groups, many Syrian refugees said that they have a hard time getting information from or communicating with service providers, with one noting, "People cannot receive treatment and do not know where to go." Refugees do not have consistent ways to determine which NGOs can help with which problems. They tend to find many UN, NGO, and government service providers unresponsive and uninformative. Having a hard time getting information "adds to stress," refugees report. When asked how they receive information, a group of refugees in Lebanon agreed that it was "by coincidence." Information routes include:

- *Information provided at registration.* When refugees register in Jordan and Lebanon, they receive information from discussions with UNHCR staff or pamphlets. Written information, of course, requires literacy to understand.
- *Word of mouth.* Most refugees we spoke with said that they receive information primarily via word of mouth from other refugees or relatives. One said: "At first when we arrived, there was no information about any assistance, however one told another and we learned that way."
- *Hotlines.* While there are advertisements for UN or NGO hotlines that refugees can call, they complain that no one picks up the phone when they call.

- *Going in person.* Refugees go in person to UN agencies, NGOs, and government facilities to get information. Going in person can be expensive because of transportation costs. "I tried calling the NGOs, but no one answers, and so I have to go physically myself," one explained. When they go to NGOs, they say that often the NGO staff takes their information, says that they will get back to them, but does not: "They do not call. There is no explanation."
- *Volunteering.* Some refugees can "volunteer" with international NGOs to work with other refugees for a small stipend (equivalent to what many earn for under-the-radar paid work). In those roles, refugees with volunteer positions with NGOs have access to information from their days spent at work, and they share this with other refugees (sometimes as part of their volunteer role). This is far more the case in Jordan than in Lebanon, where most NGOs do not want to risk the ire of government authorities for trying to employ refugees. Most of those who volunteer are often college educated. Illiterate and less-privileged refugees do not receive these positions.
- *Text messages.* Communication about reducing assistance benefits (e.g., for food assistance) often comes through text messages. Refugees noted that they receive text messages about changes in services but are baffled that they do not receive explanation about why these changes were made.

Notably, there is no online information hub or cell-phone app to share comprehensive information with the refugees, although many are educated and have access to television and smartphones. Despite substantial investments in tools to improve coordination and information among aid workers, there have not been equivalent investments in information tools for the refugees. One NGO official acknowledged: "It is hard to be transparent about the services we provide. We have more to do so that there is equal access to information and services." Refugees said that better ways to provide information to them could include field visits to communities to give information, information broadcasts on television, and activated hotlines. This lack of communication is a lost opportunity; the Syrians have high rates of literacy and capacity and could likely better meet their own needs with improved information flow.

Referrals. An important information coordination issue is referrals—when one assistance organization with one specialization notes that a refugee has need of services from another kind of organization. An example is when an NGO providing education services for children notes that parents need medical assistance for diabetes, or when a primary health care facility notes that an individual needs specialized medical care. Interviewees noted that most referrals are still manual, through personal relationships, or "chance"; some NGOs have memoranda of understanding (MOUs) to share vulnerability criteria and collaborate together. Even with a referral, refugees must repeat their stories to each new NGO, as there are no common databases. While ActivityInfo was intended to provide an online platform for sharing data, including to support referrals, NGOs would prefer a more-comprehensive referral tool with a database that contains information about each refugee. However, significant challenges would be experienced in creating such a database: UN agencies often do not share data with one another; governments view refugee data as sensitive because of demographic data on ethnicity or security considerations; refugees are sometimes afraid to share information; and providing such sensitive data to governments and multiple NGOs from multiple countries raises individual protection and security concerns. At the same time, there have been some efforts to improve coordination for referrals. For example, in Irbid, Jordan, there are caseworker-coordination meetings. Some community centers offer multiple services or coordinate access to referrals. However, a key problem with referrals is that assistance resources are so tight that, even with a referral, it can be hard for refugees to access needed assistance from the organization to which they are referred.

Evaluations. Some interviewees believed that there is "no good way of evaluating aid," due to the dearth of useful data about budgets, programs, and recipients (as previously discussed). While multiple studies have been undertaken, interviewees noted that, in many cases, they have not been shared or are not easily accessible, the evidence base is not being used as it should be, and the quality of assessments is uneven. An official in Lebanon said, "Evaluation is ad hoc." Monitoring and evaluation also tends to be about *how* activities are being done as opposed to about *what* should be done: "At the field level, they look at the quality of implementation, not the strategy."

Discussion

Strengths of Coordination Structures and Approaches

The structures that have evolved to coordinate the refugee response in Jordan and Lebanon have a number of successes and strengths, which are listed below.

Integrating "resilience" or "stabilization" goals into a refugee coordination structure. The 3RP, JRP, and LCRP set precedents because they combined a refugee response with broader sustainable goals to support host communities, tying both into national plans. JRP in particular (as the first led by a government) was described as "groundbreaking," bringing together multiple funding streams and actors into a single government-led plan. LCRP followed suit. These plans were nationally owned, in consultation with the international community, and they made it possible to overcome challenges presented by stakeholders' different goals by integrating the various efforts underway into a single planning document. While the results were not perfect, this was an important and revolutionary step forward.

Increasing government leadership. Both governments took greater leadership of the coordination process over time, with Jordan in particular noted for its effectiveness. JRP and LCRP developed planning processes in government-led responses that coordinated the work of multiple stakeholders. Those we spoke with often described Jordan as a "regional leader" as a result of its performance. Similarly, those talking about the government of Lebanon praised it for "stepping up." Furthermore, pilot efforts to coordinate with public-service needs of municipalities bring another important stakeholder into the process and may improve the representation of host communities.

Meeting needs quickly. Rolling out internationally led coordination structures enabled a fast response to the urgent needs of a large crisis. The benefit of experienced and effective international actors enabled a rapid first response that put plans and tools in place and mobilized significant funding. This made it possible to meet the basic needs of many of the most vulnerable in a number of sectors. Specifically, half of the children were provided with formal education, and most refugees were provided with at least basic health care. Sanitation systems were also expanded, with solutions put in place for informal tented settlements. Most refugees found shelter, even if that shelter is not adequate for the longer term.

Innovative approaches to some information-sharing mechanisms among aid providers. Technology has been harnessed to make many of the processes of refugee registration and aid more efficient. Iris scanning and biometrics during refugee registration help make tracking of refugees more effective. ActivityInfo makes it possible to track funded projects, and technology has helped aid providers standardize the criteria they use to assess vulnerability.

Challenges and Gaps of Coordination Structures

The coordination of the refugee response was rendered less effective by a number of factors, which are discussed below.

Unclear responsibilities among UN agencies. The UN agencies did not have clearly delineated roles and competed for leadership, especially in Lebanon. This reduced effectiveness and efficiency. Almost everyone we spoke with about the Lebanon response brought up the dysfunctional relationships among UN agencies, with particular emphasis on the relationship between UNHCR and UNOCHA. "There are such differences between UNICEF, UNESCO, and UNHCR," said one Lebanese government interviewee. Another UN interviewee told us bluntly, "We need to win the internal UN battle." A UN official in Lebanon argued, "We should look to the benefit of the people we are serving first, and a little bit less [to] the survival of organizations." The challenges evidenced in this crisis may be emblematic of problems with UN coordination more broadly. A recent review concluded that among

UN agencies there is a "fundamental problem of overlapping responsibilities" and "scatterization" (Ronald, 2011).

Differences between governments and UN agencies. There were multiple observations that the governments and UN agencies "are not on the same page," lacking coordinated procedures, with inconsistent policies. In Lebanon in particular, government officials felt that national "sovereignty" was not respected. In our view, this often had more to do with their fundamentally different goals, which lessened incentives for coordination. In addition, international personnel often felt more comfortable working with other international representatives and did not make adequate efforts to ensure that government bodies were welcomed and integrated effectively; in part, this was due to views about low government capacity. We spoke with several people who described a "wall" between the humanitarian community and the governments, impacting information flow and decisionmaking. Indeed, it was only when the governments insisted on taking a larger leadership role that international organizations began to work with them more effectively. But as governments took on larger roles, they found themselves in competition with UN agencies for leadership.

Diffusion of responsibility and limited capacity within host nation governments. Unclear divisions of responsibility within the government have been a substantial problem in Lebanon. Institutionalized political gridlock has left the country with a system in which responsibility is diffuse and decisions difficult to attain. Government officials acknowledged that political differences within the government led to contradictory actions, and line ministries sometimes intentionally did not implement the country's official policies regarding refugees. This was less of a problem in Jordan. However, in both countries, capacity constraints within some ministries prevented them from taking leadership and fully participating in responses.

Multiple time- and resource-intensive coordination structures. Both countries have experienced a proliferation of coordination structures—sector meetings, task forces, interagency meetings, ad hoc groups, and core groups. In Jordan, the UN structure runs 12 sector committees, set up at the beginning of the crisis, and the government later established 11 parallel task forces as part of JRP. Proponents explain the parallel systems thusly: The government-led set deals with strategy, and the UN structure deals with operations. In Lebanon, UNHCR and UNDP now colead nine sector committees, UNOCHA leads a parallel set of meetings, and there is a quartet of leaders of UN agencies (intended to reduce tensions among UN agency leadership and coordinate differing policies). Both countries have an additional set of structures for international NGOs (in which local NGOs are not included). Interviewees with multiple roles in both countries commented on "aid worker's disease," meaning that there was "too much coordination with too little output," with too many meetings, too many structures, too much overhead, and inefficient use of time and funds. Several NGO officials estimated that they spend half of their working hours in coordination meetings. There were repeated observations that these structures were consuming significant amounts of funding through salaries and overhead.

Lack of a culture of accountability to plans. Several interviewees observed an absence of a culture of accountability to plans, both among international stakeholders and local ones. Several note that much less in-person coordination would be needed if there were detailed strategies with which activities were aligned. Interviewees observed that, in many cases, funding and programs were not captured within plans; donors did not adhere to frameworks and instead worked bilaterally; NGOs went around the frameworks to find individual funding for the programs that they wanted to carry out; and governments lacked a means of capturing funding and programs within their planning, not transparently accounting for what had been provided. One interviewee summed it up: "There would be less need for constant coordination if we had the tools and if we were all more closely behind a strategic direction."

Coordination among donors. Donors' roles in coordinating policy are not commensurate with funds that they provide. Among the donors, there is little consistent policy coordination or pooling of advocacy. While countries sometimes develop common positions, this is done in an ad hoc manner. While additional funding would certainly help the response, so would certain policy changes enabling more-effective administration of aid. Donors could work together to advocate such change. Interviewees noted areas where donor advocacy could have impact, in particular, in registration and livelihoods policies. One donor representative said about the lack of policy coordination or donor advocacy with host governments: "There is no systematic pressure from the internationally funded efforts." Another noted, "With all this money, we [donors] should have stronger leverage with the government." Representatives explained this by arguing that donors are used to working with the host governments bilaterally rather than in concert with one another. Several donor representatives commented that their country's contributions were not enough to gain leverage with either the governments or the UN system, but they acknowledged that donors working together would enjoy more leverage. Moreover, many felt that Western and Gulf donors were disconnected from one another and perhaps working at cross-purposes.

Insular coordination among the international community. While the UN system and international NGOs coordinate with one another extensively, coordination links are much weaker with the governments and local NGOs. This creates a "wall" between international aid providers on one side and government and local NGOs on the other. National governments are not consistently involved in internationally led coordination structures, and local NGOs are marginalized. Several local NGOs expressed frustration at perceived exclusion from International NGO Forums. Some international NGO officials acknowledged that, in providing a rapid response, the international NGO community did not spend enough effort to include and build capacity of local entities. There is almost no coordination with faith-based groups or with the refugees themselves. According to interviewees, the response has yet to transition to truly involving national civil society: "We undermined building the capacities of local NGOs. I understand that because of speed, you can't wait for capacity, but you can do it in parallel, to pass on knowledge and skills." Gulf donors and local faith-based NGOs remain largely outside of coordination structures.

Misaligned incentives between governments and NGOs. Government officials in both countries expressed some reticence about the roles of NGOs, describing them as creating "chaos" characterized by a mix of programs uncoordinated with government priorities. They also said that they lack visibility into what international NGOs are doing, identified understanding what NGO activities were underway as a priority, and complained that NGOs often prefer programs that are visible for the NGO, rather than coordinating with line ministries about their needs. At the same time, among international NGOs, some view government decisions as "unpredictable" and not communicated; they expressed particular frustration with government policies that made it difficult to obtain visas for additional international staff.

Little coordination with refugees. As previously discussed, there is little coordination with the refugees themselves. No refugee representatives are included in any of the UN- or government-led coordination structures. In focus groups, refugees said that they had a hard time registering their concerns or getting information. The refugee-response organizations cannot hire refugees because of labor laws in Lebanon and Jordan, although some organizations take them as "volunteers." Impediments to coordinating with the refugees include an urgent time frame, language barriers, capacity of both aid workers and refugees, and lack of structures to include them. One NGO representative in Lebanon said: "A challenge is that we decide on behalf of the refugees. Coordination groups are of stakeholders, but never were the refugees consulted about priorities for the year, not even for validation."

Poor fiscal planning and tracking. The 3RP budgets were based on coordinated consensus between government and international stakeholders, rather than on needs assessments, options appraisals comparing cost effectiveness and efficiency, or prioritization in the face of budget constraints. Moreover, accounting is complicated because of multiple types of funding streams from multiple entities and few centralized ways to aggregate their activities. There is inconsistency in how humanitarian- and development-aid streams are classified. This is not to imply that donor funds are too high—even with greater efficiencies, current funding is likely insufficient. However, it would go a lot further if fiscal planning and tracking were improved.

Increased costs due to heavy involvement of international organizations. International agencies and NGOs receive the bulk of funding. This is because of donor preference (some of it political and unlikely to change) and tradition. The result is that large amounts of funds are spent on staff time (including for coordination), high overhead rates, and financing being passed through a long chain of stakeholders, with additional costs incurred at each stage. There are multiple layers of pass-throughs, with money circulating among multiple agencies before it gets to the refugees or the host communities.

Weak mechanisms for evaluating aid. A dearth of useful data about budgets, programs, and recipients makes evaluation a challenge. Even where data exist, the evidence base is not being used as it should be, and the quality of assessments is uneven. Evaluation ends up ad hoc and focused on how activities are conducted rather than what they do.

Referrals hampered by gaps in data sharing. Although there has been real progress on data sharing between aid providers, one area that continues to experience gaps is referrals, which would require broadly accessible databases that include information about each refugee. This would be a challenge because the data are sensitive, refugees are wary of sharing it and having it be shared, and UN agencies themselves often have difficulty sharing data, even with one another.

Weak information flow to refugees. Despite substantial investments in tools to improve coordination and information among aid workers, there have not been equivalent investments in information tools for the refugees. Refugees receive limited information, which rarely explains why changes to benefits or services have been made. As a result, they view aid as capricious and confusing. For many refugees, efforts to obtain information from UN, NGO, and government service providers are often unsuccessful and almost always frustrating. Aid flows toward refugees without including them in coordination.

Summary

Early efforts in both Jordan and Lebanon suffered from development based on the experience of aid efforts conducted in rural areas and camps in poorer countries and failed states, rather than among middle-income populations in urban areas. This led to an expensive parallel set of structures with assistance and investment in UN agencies and international NGOs, rather than in host-country institutions. This structure, while useful early in the crisis, is proving to be an unsustainable use of funds in the longer term.

JRP and LCRP were milestones in approaches to coordination. JRP and LCRP enabled a stronger host-government role and thus more-effective integration of host-government priorities with those of the international aid agencies. The result was that coordination structures brought together programs to assist refugees with local development efforts, which also provide support to host communities. They also made possible the recognition of a longer time frame for the crisis and thus for assistance programs. However, confusion remains about how the principles expressed in these strategy documents are or should be translated into roles, responsibilities, and budgeted programming. It is also not always clear what the governments are capable of doing and are willing to do and what the roles of the international aid community will be going forward. Conflicting priorities among stakeholders and turf battles among UN agencies, between the governments and the UN system, and between international NGOs and local NGOs, have led to inefficiencies. These inefficiencies may appear to be coordination failures but often simply stem from divergent viewpoints, goals, and priorities.

Funding has not been transparent, and longer-term planning and sustainability have yet to develop into budgeting and programming. Budgets lack prioritization and options analyses, and there are few plans to transition to longer-term management of service provision for refugees and host communities. Because new coordination structures have been added to the old, the resulting system is unwieldy, expensive, and highly inefficient, wasting both time and money. We heard many calls for a new aid model with less time and resources spent on coordination.

CHAPTER FOUR

Recommendations

Syria's civil war has displaced half its population, with eight million people having fled to other parts of the country and nearly five million refugees abroad. The refugee crisis has largely been what is termed "urban," with most refugees living among host communities rather than in camps. Jordan, Lebanon, and other host countries have generously opened their borders and offered their increasingly burdened public services to those fleeing Syria. UN agencies and NGOs have provided important support to meet urgent needs with donor funding. Yet, despite dedicated people working around the clock to help, the current refugee response in Jordan and Lebanon is not meeting needs in education, health care, shelter, water and sanitation, and livelihoods.

The best way to improve the circumstances of the refugees would be to stabilize Syria so that refugees could return home. But the events of the last five years indicate that planning cannot be based on the hope that this can be done. Rather, both the region and the world must prepare for ongoing instability in Syria for the foreseeable future and the resulting protracted refugee situation. This creates an even-greater imperative to develop and coordinate improved solutions so that refugees can have stable and legal access to shelter, employment, water and sanitation, health care, and education so that host countries have the resources they need on the front lines of this crisis. This report has considered how coordination among the main stakeholders—governments, donors, UN agencies, NGOs, and the refugees themselves—has enabled access to services for the refugees to date, and where it has been unable to meet needs. Therefore, in consideration of the protracted urban nature of the refugee crisis, this chapter offers recommendations for new approaches that emphasize transferring responsibility, as well as donor resources, to host governments and national programs. Recommendations aim to improve coordination of the Syrian refugee response in Jordan and Lebanon; some recommendations may generalize to the other Syrian refugee host countries and to other urban refugee crises. (The actors who would implement the recommendations are set in bold-face type.)

The recommendations presented here will be difficult to implement: They require changes to funding models, working relationships, roles and responsibilities, and planning time frames, all of which are meant to be executed in the midst of crisis. Although the war in Syria has already lasted years, it is difficult for many stakeholders in Jordan and Lebanon to publicly acknowledge that the refugee crisis and its effects will continue longer than anticipated. This is exacerbated by competing visions about the right courses of action and resource constraints. The governments of both Jordan and Lebanon lack financial transparency and face capacity shortages. Current aid structures and processes are ingrained and hard to change. Between donor and host countries, there are other pressing bilateral issues that can have higher precedence than specific refugee-related policy. Lebanon is particularly challenging for U.S. policymakers because of restrictions in place on working with the government as long as Hezbollah is part of it.

But the reality is that the situation has gotten worse over time, and numbers of refugees are rising, not shrinking.

These challenges are outweighed by the tremendous risks and costs posed by the status quo. Failure to improve the effectiveness of the management and coordination of the refugee response means a much-broader failure. This includes, first of all, five million refugees who cannot meet their basic needs. This, in turn, creates longer-term economic and societal risks, which may last generations, given the educational gaps that face at least half of the refugee children and the lack of opportunities for refugee (and host-community) youth. The inadequacy of the response in Jordan and Lebanon is partly responsible for the further waves of migration to Europe. Second, Jordan and Lebanon are under strain, as their governments are providing what they can in the way of education, health care, and more to the refugees without adequate donor funding, degrading previously robust public services. In time, this could threaten stability in those countries, as host communities become more frustrated with the effects on their own circumstances, as demonstrated by public protests in Beirut in 2015 over overburdened sanitation systems that were no longer able to collect garbage. Third, continuing reliance on outdated approaches to the refugee response creates and perpetuates expensive and ineffective parallel services. By increasing costs, it contributes further to difficulties in meeting needs in education, health care, sanitation, and more. Investment in internationally managed services now, as opposed to national services, will not leave the capacity behind into the future. In addition, creation of separate facilities for education, health care, and more has the potential to further divide societies that are more fragile because of the civil war and refugee crisis.

At the same time, there are opportunities to take advantage of in implementing these recommendations. There are high levels of individual capacity and education in both Lebanon and Jordan and among the Syrians. People are motivated and want to help. The substantial existing institutional capacity in Jordan and Lebanon creates a solid foundation to build on. The UN system and NGOs bring experience and capacity, and our interviews for this report revealed a recognition on the part of many, if not most, stakeholders of the need for new and different ways of ensuring effectiveness.

While current models for the refugee response have gone a long way in meeting some needs, they will not be able to expand services as quickly as needed to as many people as needed and sustain those services into the future. This is why change is required.

Improve Donor Coordination by Creating a "Contact Group" for the Syrian Refugee Response Led by the U.S. Department of State

The Syrian refugee crisis will affect the Middle East, Europe, and the world for at least a generation. Political and diplomatic leadership is needed to improve responses and mitigate the challenges presented by the influx of people to countries near and far from Syria's borders. While additional funding is important, additional policy leadership is also needed. While sometimes donor policy priorities are aligned, the largest donors have not formally coordinated policy priorities for the refugee response in the Middle East. Currently, no ongoing formal donor policy coordination mechanisms for the Syrian refugee situation exist. In addition to UN leadership, there is need for greater leadership from leading nations. The United States has been the largest donor (more than the next three largest donors combined), and its predominance as a donor, as well as its diplomatic leadership of cease-fire negotiations within Syria, makes it a good candidate to take greater refugee-policy leadership with other donor countries, the governments of the host countries, and UN agencies.

Much as the U.S. Department of State initiated and led the "Contact Group," a six-country leadership group during the Balkan wars, we recommend that the U.S. Department of State initiate a similar Contact Group for the Syrian refugee crisis. The Contact Group in the Balkans was effective, as it provided a means for large donors to first agree on positions bilaterally, then in small groups, and then at larger meetings, through gradually expanding coordination structures. In the Balkans, a Western "quint" of five nations met with Russia as the sixth nation. The Contact Group was the driving force in getting problems solved. It built consensus from the ground up and in concentric circles.

The proposed Syrian Refugee Response Contact Group would be a flexible body that enables concerned leading countries to coordinate their positions prior to meeting with host governments and UN agencies. Specifically, the Syrian Refugee Response Contact Group might meet at the Assistant Secretary level on a quarterly basis. The Contact Group would:

- Consider refugee issues both at national levels and at a regional level.
- Harness donors' own short-term humanitarian and longer-term development funds in a coordinated effort.
- Integrate resources and policies into realistic funded plans.

- Develop common priorities and solutions.
- Leverage donor funding to help host governments implement sound policy solutions.
- Take coordinated donor positions to host governments and leading UN agencies.

The United States has offered to host the UN Summit on Refugees and Migrants (taking place in September 2016), as well as a High-Level Meeting of the UN General Assembly Plenary on Addressing Large Movements of Refugees and Migrants. Preparation for these events could provide an opportunity to begin to move forward on this recommendation.

There are two options for structuring the U.S.-led Syrian Refugee Response Contact Group. One option would be to build on the existing coordinating body of nations that have worked through Syria's cease fire, including Russia, Iran, Saudi Arabia, and others. However, the nations involved in the cease fire have not been the most active in addressing the refugee crisis. An alternative option would be a parallel coordinating function for the refugee crisis specifically that involves the major players among the main refugee-response donors (the United States, the EU, the United Kingdom, Germany, and Kuwait), the main host countries (Turkey, Lebanon, Jordan, and Iraq), and others deemed central by participants. The United States could first work closely with key allies and partners among the donors to make decisions, and then coordinate with other countries involved. This approach also would allow for interaction with the coordination involved in the cease fire, as needed.

This recommendation does not underestimate the political challenges inherent in bringing together countries with disparate interests and positions in a complex and polarized situation—rather, it is intended as a means to address these problems. This is a particularly complicated situation because of the numbers of countries involved and their diverse interests—the United States, Western European donors, Gulf States, Russia, Iran, and the host countries. The continued difficult circumstances of the refugee crisis present an urgent case for additional leadership and coordinated decisionmaking. The United States is well placed to play that leadership role.

Embed a Ten-Year Outlook in the Planning Process for the Refugee Responses in Jordan and Lebanon

Planning to date has been short term, with a maximum time frame of up to two years. However, there will likely be a substantial Syrian refugee presence in Jordan and Lebanon for at least the next decade. Interviewees indicated that the short-term plans that have relied on short-term donor commitments and international organizations offering parallel services are inadequate. Under **U.S. leadership, the "Contact Group" and its members** should provide impetus for **the governments of Jordan and Lebanon, UNHCR, and other UN agencies** to develop medium-term plans for provision of public services to refugees.

Given the extensive unmet needs among the refugees, the continuing nature of the crisis, current budgets that primarily support the UN system and international NGOs rather than Jordanian and Lebanese institutions, and the low proportion of the UN donor request for 2015 that was funded, a new set of prioritized plans is needed, with accompanying budgets. The 3RP was meant to provide planning for 2015 and 2016. If a new planning process were to be implemented in 2016, it could be ready for 2017 onward.

There are challenges to creating such a ten-year outlook. Publicly planning for the medium term is politically unpalatable for the host governments. PRM receives its budgets from Congress only in annual cycles. UNHCR is set up to focus on short-term refugee crises. At the same time, to not consider the medium-term means to continue to have a patchwork of temporary programs that will not meet needs. It also perpetuates a "state within a state," with UN agencies managing some level of public services (that were meant to be temporary) into the future in Jordan and Lebanon, while government services continue to degrade. The Syrian refugee crisis has already passed five years. Protracted refugee crises often last decades. Failure to plan accordingly cannot help but mean much broader failure.

While creating ten-year specific plans may not be feasible, at the least, planning should assume that a ten-year horizon is possible, even if plan specifics are only detailed for a shorter term. This is made more plausible by the increasing recognition of all involved—including the host governments—that temporary time frames are insufficient, and we have seen steps toward multiyear planning.

One way of managing this would be to call on **United Nations agencies, host countries**, and other critical stakeholders to develop plans that take into account multiple scenarios, including one of a near-term return for many refugees as well as those of varying numbers of refugees staying in their host countries for a number of years. This planning can include publicly stated goals of getting the refugees home as soon as possible, but it can also allow for the possibility that the best case will not become reality.

The United States should ensure that its own crisis planning is done jointly by **USAID and PRM**, incorporating both refugee and host-country development needs. While PRM may not be in a position to do ten-year planning, it can adopt a ten-year outlook and begin plans that set up the people of the region for future self-reliance. The **U.S. Congress** should also recognize that this refugee crisis is not a yearlong event and allow for long-term planning in its budget allocations.

All of these long-term planning efforts should, of course, be carefully coordinated through both existing and recommended processes. To engage the governments of Lebanon and Jordan in longer-term planning, PRM, USAID, UN agencies, and other donors should conduct planning in concert with financial commitments for assistance that incorporate development needs in Lebanon and Jordan into the refugee response. **NGOs** seeking funding from UN agencies and donors should indicate how their proposed efforts fit into plans with a ten-year horizon, plans that are the results of these multiyear planning processes.

Create a Funding Plan with Ten-Year Vision

Jordan, Lebanon, and other regional host countries are providing the world a great good by opening their borders and offering their services to refugees. To enable them to continue doing so, **the United States and other donors** should support them with resources for service provision.

If plans are medium term, budgets and investments should also consider a medium-term time frame to enable stable access to reliable funding. As part of the "Contact Group" process, we recommend that **the United States and other donors** support planning with a ten-year funding vision (to the extent feasible) and coordinate with one another to ensure that their plans are aligned. The ten-year funding vision should also include a reduction of external funding over time, with planning of transition to local funding sources to avoid circumstances such as those of UNRWA, in which donors and the UN have taken responsibility for a refugee population for a half-century. This should include the following steps:

- **A coordinated PRM-USAID funding and investment plan.** For the U.S. Department of State, this could mean coordinating with USAID to develop **joint PRM-USAID plans** that take into account refugee and host-country development needs, as well as how these could shift over time.
- **Reliance on the Syrian refugees themselves as a primary source of funding**. Even if there were dramatic increases in donor funding for the refugee response, the amounts would still not be enough to support the refugees' personal needs and their use of public services. Syrians need to have the means to support themselves financially and contribute to their own public services, for example, through paying wage taxes. **Host-government** employment policies that make it possible for the refugees to support themselves, pay for their own shelter, and pay taxes to support the public services that they need in health, education, water and sanitation, and more, are crucial. Specifically, this means that host governments must develop evidence-based labor-market policies

intended to enable refugees to work and contribute positively to the economies of Jordan and Lebanon, while protecting them from exploitation and maintaining a commitment that the refugees will return to Syria once conditions are stable.

- **Loans to the host governments.** Other sources of funding may include the World Bank, private sector, or other loans for needed public-sector infrastructure investment and expansion in schools, hospitals, housing, and sanitation.
- **Public-private partnerships.** Jordan and Lebanon could also explore creative financing ideas, such as the use of public-private partnerships (in which the private sector finances and builds infrastructure and rents it to the government), which have been successfully used in other countries such as Egypt, Spain, the United Kingdom, and elsewhere when governments need ways to mobilize capital for public infrastructure investment.

Evaluate Current Plans and Develop New Plans in Jordan and Lebanon for Each Sector (1) Based on Needs Assessments, (2) Using the "Approach Areas" as a Framework, and (3) Transferring Responsibility to National Entities as Appropriate

If the United States and other donors shift from support primarily for UN and NGO parallel programs to efforts that build the capacity of host countries and local NGOs, they may help to create integrated, lower-cost, and more-sustainable services. It may also help host communities adapt to the refugee presence by expanding and improving public services that both refugees and host communities rely on. In other words, where feasible, implementation, and thus a large part of planning, should be the role of **governments and local entities, with U.S. and other donor support**.

The current 3RP planning process, while a substantial improvement over past approaches, lacks analysis of options for meeting needs, outcomes, and cost effectiveness, with its budgets instead based on coordinated consensus among stakeholders and funding recipients. Sustaining a long-term refugee response requires using donor funding in significantly more-efficient, effective, and targeted ways. Support needs to be sufficient to meet refugee needs in ways that strengthen capacity of host-nation governments and communities, rather than supplementing refugee assistance with similar, internationally led programs for host communities as "compensation." Assistance that strengthens systems and infrastructure in areas most strained by refugee needs will work better in the long term. This includes education, health care, and water and sanitation infrastructure. Programs should be selected and evaluated on this basis.

In Chapter Two, we described a set of five approach areas that affect coordination and provision of public services for refugees in urban areas: time frame, nature of services, leadership, funding recipients, and focus. This framework could be useful for assessing current plans for each sector and the overall response. This, in turn, will enable coordinating bodies to establish realistic expectations of each stakeholder, enable them to invest in the areas where they bring unique value added, and fill remaining gaps. There is no one right answer about what the balance in each sector and crisis might be. This will depend on the context of each specific situation, which will evolve over time. As this is a refugee population, particular issues specific to refugee needs, such as protection and registration, should remain managed by international humanitarian actors, but, over time, as much aid as is feasible should transition to the responsibility of Jordan and Lebanon, with adequate oversight.

In Table 4.1, we propose a set of criteria for **UN agencies, donors, and governments** to consider in developing new ten-year strategies for the sectors going forward. (We note that some of the criteria depend on levels of government capacity, which may be difficult for donors, UN agencies, or the governments to judge. These issues may be addressed on a case-by-case basis by negotiation among parties.) This may make it possible to:

- Directly support national service delivery rather than provision of services by UN agencies and NGOs when appropriate and feasible.

Table 4.1
Criteria for Determining Strategies Across Approach Areas

Time Frame	
Conduct Short-Term Planning	**Conduct Medium-Term Planning**
• During first two years of crisis • When needs are urgent and for meeting emergency needs • When fast action is required to address problems	• After two years of crisis or as soon as it is clear that the crisis may be protracted • After major political junctions that indicate solution is distant • To sustain needs • When needs are more than short-term

Nature of Services	
Create New or Parallel Services When:	**Use Existing Government Services or Strengthen Them When:**
• Local services cannot meet needs quickly • Necessary local services do not exist • Reliance on local services would crowd out host-country citizens and expansion is not feasible/not yet possible • Parallel systems will be temporary to meet immediate needs in line with above • When international funding and skills can be higher quality and more cost effective • Services are for needs specific to refugees	• The government could provide services more effectively or efficiently over the long term • The government has robust capacity that could be scaled up or improved with investment • The government will need capacity in the long term • There is a need to rely on services long term • Donor funding is time limited

Table 4.1—Continued

Leadership	
Rely on International Leadership	**Facilitate National Leadership**
• When rapid action is required to address problems and host countries cannot respond • When complex coordination among multiple stakeholders is needed and host countries cannot provide that • In the beginning of the crisis, if host country capacity is insufficient • When the international aid community can mobilize capacities that local entities cannot on an urgent basis • On issues related to needs specific to the refugees and not host-country populations (e.g., protection, food assistance)	• When national governments and civil societies have the capacity for service provision and coordination • When national governments have the political will • To sustain needs
Funding Recipients or Channels	
Fund UN Agencies and INGOs	**Fund Governments and LNGOs**
• For the services that they provide • For roles that cannot be done by the government, private sector, refugees, or civil societies • For sectors in which parallel service provision is needed • When accountability systems within governments cannot be created	• In proportion to the prioritized services that they provide • For roles that can be done by the government and local NGOs • For national public services that the governments have integrated for refugees (e.g., education, health, sanitation) • When the government has accountability systems in place to manage funding
Focus	
Focus on Refugees	**Focus on Refugees and/Within Host Communities**
• For needs particular to the refugees • In the beginning of the crisis	• When refugees and host communities rely on shared services and resources • To ameliorate the pressure created by refugee presence on the host communities

- Better optimize the balance of roles among UN agencies, governments, and NGOs to leverage priorities and skills.
- Align funding to entities in proportion with their responsibilities (in particular, by providing funding for national public services when provided by governments).
- Better use NGO capacity to provide temporary services, capacity-development support, information dissemination, and case management, with parallel service provision only when absolutely needed.
- Inform effective program evaluation, carried out by third parties rather than aid providers, and based on objective and previously agreed criteria, to help ensure that funds are spent wisely.

Invest in Capacity of Governments, Municipalities, National Civil Society, and the Private Sector to Take Greater Roles

A significant risk is that, as funding dwindles over time and international humanitarian actors leave, the capacity to manage independently in Jordan and Lebanon is not left behind. A medium-term plan, with responsibility transferred to nationally led integrated services, requires a deliberative **donor and UN strategy** to build capacity of Jordanian and Lebanese institutions, with recognition that not all responsibility will be able to be transferred because of refugee-specific needs that are the UN's mandate to address, government capacity, and/or political will. Governments of Jordan and Lebanon are already offering services (in particular in health care, education, and sanitation/water). The international donor community should take it on itself to enable them to continue by supporting these expansions and improving quality through donor funding and technical assistance. We recommend some of the following steps in transitioning responsibility and resources to entities in Jordan and Lebanon:

- **Operations.** Make three-year donor commitments to fund staff salaries at public institutions to expand services to accommodate

Syrians over time. For example, for Jordan's Ministry of Education and Lebanon's MEHE, donors should set up a fund to directly pay for salaries of teachers, including Syrian refugees who were teachers in Syria.

- **Infrastructure.** Fund buildings, renovations, supplies, and equipment. For example, for both Jordan and Lebanon, donors should invest in upgraded sanitation and water systems, clinics and health care equipment, and school buildings to handle the greater numbers of people.
- **Institutional systems.** Build national and local institutional capacity through donor-funded secondment of technical experts, training on aspects of managing the crisis, creating data systems, providing ongoing technical advice, and developing standards and policies.
- **Inclusion.** Build capacity in local NGOs by including them in International NGO Forums in Jordan and Lebanon. Structure meetings of such forums to enable local NGO participation, such as offering interpretation of Arabic, inviting local NGOs to contribute to agenda development, and organizing pre-meetings or orientations for local NGOs new to the international system. Donors or UN agencies can provide proposal training and require local NGO partners on international NGO projects—not just local staff, but local institutions.

Invest in Government Financial Accountability Systems

Working through governments creates challenges for financial accountability. It is important to ensure that money goes where it is meant to and that it is spent as intended. Therefore, we also recommend that effective accounting and transparency measures be a requirement for U.S. support and that the United States, in its donor-leadership role, work to make these measures the standard across every relief and development effort. This could include the **United States or other donors** funding development of accountability systems within governments to allay concerns about transparency and requiring evidence of accountability in exchange for direct funding of government services for the refugees. There are several options for ensuring financial accountability.

- **Use of professional third-party auditing firms.** When money is allocated, hire third-party auditing firms to have oversight of use of funds.
- **Paying for performance.** Pay for specific line items that support goals in the sectors. Tie money to measurable results that can be validated as a requirement for further support (e.g., paying for specific and verified hospital and health services or teacher salaries).
- **Project Management Units.** Emulate the Millennium Challenge Corporation's Project Management Units to help ensure accountability within ministries. Project Management Units are public-private partnerships between government and civil society through which funds flow and which manage money for a particular purpose. They are inside the governments, are responsive for tracking funds, deliver particular objectives, and are transparent. They are headed by an official and buttressed by an outside team of experts. For example, Project Management Units could be put into the education, health care, and public works ministries.
- **Direct contracting.** Hire contractors for infrastructure projects and pay contractors directly for performance.

While improved financial accountability is important for both Jordan and Lebanon, Lebanon presents the additional consideration in that Congress forbids direct funding to Lebanon as long as Hezbollah is part of the government. Lebanon is providing education through its public schools, health care through its public hospitals, and sanitation and water in its cities. If Lebanon is willing to provide these services, then there should be ways for donors to enable expansion of these services—but with accountability that money is spent as intended. In Lebanon's case, instead of giving money to the government to distribute, donors who decide not to fund government coffers directly could allocate money for very specific purposes, and then have it managed by a third-party bank (e.g., for paying teacher or other salaries). Support for such services could be enabled with a third party that administers funds or contracts, thus eliminating the need to directly fund the central government. If donors aimed to fund public-service operational costs (such as salaries of additional teachers or nurses), funding flows could be managed by an international bank with a local presence and with third-party auditing. Multi-donor trust funds could also be modified to address other donor concerns.

Streamline the International Coordination Structures and Funding Channels in Jordan and Lebanon

Medium-term planning guided by the **U.S.-led "Contact Group"** should include a vision for the international coordination structure and funding channels over the coming years, with priority on strengthening government-led initiatives when capacity is sufficient; increasing the role of refugees, municipalities, and the private sector; and reducing the numbers of international staff in international humanitarian coordination structures.

First, the current coordination structure—with a proliferation of working groups, task forces, and sector leads and heavy reliance on international staff in UN agencies and international NGOs—is not financially sustainable into the future. Moreover, many public-service provision functions now carried out by international organizations could be performed by entities in Jordan and Lebanon. **UN agencies with responsibility for the refugee response, in collaboration with donors and the governments of Jordan and Lebanon**, should develop plans for the response that include concrete goals and paths to transition responsibilities to local entities. This includes providing capacity-building support (as needed) to ensure that local entities have the skills and the resources to take over.

Second, coordination itself (among **UN agencies, NGOs, and governments**) should be refocused from frequent tactical interactions to collaborative strategy and planning. With well-designed strategy and implementation plans in place and all stakeholders signed on, coordination can work to the plans, limiting the need for many coordination meetings.

Third, while donors may prefer to outsource administration of contracting to UN agencies, to make the best use of scarce budgets, **donors and UN agencies** can and should direct funding more efficiently. This means using fewer pass-throughs, with funding going to entities in proportion to their responsibilities.

Establish and Maintain Clear UN Agency Roles and Responsibilities

In both countries, and in particular in Lebanon, multiple interviewees spoke of myriad problems in coordination that stem from UN internal politics, with unclear roles among agencies, turf battles, redundant coordination structures led by UNHCR and UNOCHA, lack of data and information sharing between UN agencies, inconsistent UN policies, the cost of overhead of multiple agencies, and more. These internal UN political issues confuse the governments, hamper efficiency, and waste resources. In this crisis, and in other refugee crises going forward, the **UN Interagency Standing Committee** should reconsider how it allocates responsibilities in humanitarian crises, define clear leadership and roles among UN agencies, determine the right number of UN agencies that need to be involved, and avoid placing "too many cooks in the kitchen." The simple presence of a Humanitarian Coordinator (who was meant to coordinate among UN agencies) has proven insufficient, suggesting a need for a stronger UN institutional response. This said, this recommendation is specific to the requirement to better coordinate the refugee response. As such, we do not address the potential institutional implications within the headquarters of the UN system of such changes. In cases in which there are reports of coordination problems, the **Interagency Standing Committee** should develop a mechanism for resolving such issues.

Include Refugees in Coordination of the Refugee Response and Improve Communication to Refugees

While helping refugees is the purpose of the refugee response, refugees are not included in planning and coordination. While there has been innovative use of technology and communication tools for aid workers, there are also few avenues for communicating with refugees consistently or gaining their input about overarching needs and priorities. Targeted information would help enable refugees to be more self-reliant in meeting their needs. We recommend implementing concrete measures to involve the refugees in the refugee response, including both ways of pushing information out to them as well as gaining their inputs to the policy process. This can include a number of steps.

- **UN- and government-led coordination structures** should establish mechanisms, such as refugee advisory boards, with broad representation across gender, age, and social class, to enable refugee input into decisions and planning for government services and NGO program designs and needs assessments.
- **Donors and UN agencies** should fund and develop a communication plan to provide information to the refugees. This could include television announcements, a refugee information-portal website in Arabic (much like UNHCR's portal), apps for smart phones about how to access services, and additional paper brochures about services. These could include updates about services or assistance, contact information for key services, information about their rights, links to forms, referral pathways, and more.
- **Donors** should increase funding for the use of community-based hubs (to be managed by **municipalities or national civil society**) that serve as one-stop shops for refugees to get information, coordinate referrals, and get help with making appointments. Community hubs could also be places where refugees interact with local host communities. (In implementing such approaches, aid providers and community leaders must be wary of the dangers of refugees or local entities capturing such programs on behalf of political parties or factions.)

- When developing terms of reference for implementers (UN agencies or NGOs), **donors** should reward programs for effective inclusion of refugees in their activities, both through refugee boards to review aid priorities and through reliance on refugee skill sets to help fill service gaps (e.g., in health care, education, administration, labor).
- **Donor-funded programs** should require hiring refugees themselves, in addition to international, Jordanian, and Lebanese staff. This will serve as a means to include refugee perspectives, increase effectiveness of programming, provide livelihoods for some refugees, and build Syrian refugee experience so that skills are available for similar needs when Syria is stabilized and needs to be rebuilt.

Roll Out a Municipality Prioritization and Coordination Effort

Within the shift to managing the refugee response at the national and local levels with donor funding, we recommend to **donors and UN agencies** a focus on working with **municipalities**, as well as with the national governments. While many efforts should remain at the national level with national government agencies, there are other issues that are local. We recommend a donor-funded program to convene leadership from municipalities and representatives of the refugees who reside in those municipalities to develop a priority list of investments to enable communities to manage the presence of the refugees. Examples discussed earlier in the report showed that municipal priorities can be innovative and may be cost effective, such as installing additional streetlights to improve security and investments in public waste management and water. Finding ways to meet community needs may also ameliorate some of the tensions between the host communities and refugees.

To start, with approval from the national governments, a few municipalities with demonstrated track records for leadership might be selected in each country. Programs could then convene councils of municipal leadership, officials from key public sectors (e.g., from education, health, WASH), and refugees. With facilitation from donor-funded programs, the councils could develop prioritized lists of investment or support needs for consideration of donors such as PRM, USAID, or others. Based on lessons learned from these experiences, such efforts could be expanded.

Engage the Private Sector in Coordination in Relevant Areas

The private sector is not engaged in coordination in the sectors. UN agencies and international NGOs take on roles typically associated with the private sector, such as in housing, banking, employment, construction of needed infrastructure, and availability of food and other needed items. In Lebanon, much of the health care and education provisions for citizens are provided by the private sector. As both Lebanon and Jordan have thriving private sectors and functioning markets, there are opportunities to find creative or more-efficient ways of addressing some of the medium-term problems by engaging the private sector. They include

- involving private-sector representatives in **sector working groups** (such as chambers of commerce or other groups, as it is important that such efforts avoid privileging particular companies)
- releasing **UN or donor** tenders for certain types of service provision to solicit proposals for more effectively or efficiently meeting service needs
- engaging banking, accounting, or audit firms (by **donors or UN agencies**) to develop plans to streamline funding channels while ensuring accountability and transparency of fund use
- exploring public-private partnerships for building some of the **donor or UN**-funded infrastructure in health, education, sanitation, and housing that is needed

- exploring how the private sector, in particular in Lebanon, can be relied upon to expand capacity in education and health care (e.g., with education vouchers or health care insurance).

Seek Opportunities to Coordinate Both Refugee Needs and Host-Country Development Goals in Program Design

To the host communities, the presence of the refugees is viewed largely in terms of drawbacks, such as higher rents, lower wages, and crowded public services. However, the refugees also bring benefits with them, such as their skills, their labor, their demand for purchases in the local economies, and the aid money that comes with their presence. Most efforts to help the refugees have focused on the refugees, and efforts to help the host communities have been separate and through development channels. This report found a number of approaches in which a single intervention helped both refugees and host communities. One example is the NRC's program to pay for additions to host-community housing in exchange for housing refugees. These win-win strategies are keys to developing effective and efficient programs and also reducing resentment between the two communities. While the governments of Jordan and Lebanon have tried to accomplish this by mandating that a percentage of all funding goes to their own vulnerable citizens, this approach may not be the most efficient or effective in helping the refugees, building national capacity, or enabling longer-term planning. As programs are rolled out, a framing question should be: How can programs be designed to help both communities? The answer to this question will vary by circumstance, but below are examples of such win-win activities as well as new ideas that **all funders—whether host governments, donor governments, or international organizations**—might consider:

- investing in infrastructure expansion for the host communities
- hiring refugees as workers on donor-funded infrastructure projects for schools, hospitals, etc.; labor for such projects was imported in both countries before the crisis

- developing standards for the refugee response that also benefit the host community. For example, as UNICEF was investing in bathroom facilities for overcrowded schools, it developed standards for school bathrooms and seconded staff to the Ministry of Education to implement these facility standards more widely across Jordan. In Lebanon, mental health care standards developed for refugees in clinics were also rolled out through the Ministry of Public Health for citizens of Lebanon
- conducting a labor-market study about how refugees can contribute to economies.

APPENDIX A

Coordination in Six Sectors

Five sectors identified by Syrian refugees as most important to them in a 2013 UNHCR survey were employment, shelter, WASH, health, and education (Crisp et al., 2013). To this list of sectors identified by refugees as important, we add the legal sector, which affects the other sectors. In this Appendix, we discuss coordination of assistance to refugees in Jordan and Lebanon in the context of each of these sectors. We also review how the framework of approach areas (time frame, nature of services, leadership, funding recipients, and focus) outlined in Chapter Two applies in each sector. For the discussion about funding recipients, we note that the available budget documentation discusses funding recipients at the aggregate levels, with $4.5 billion of the total requested 3RP budget to UN agencies and NGOs and with $1 billion to governments, but does not break these numbers down in most cases by sector. Instead, budgets of the 3RP, JRP, and LCRP are broken down by "refugee" and "resilience" in JRP, and "humanitarian" and "stabilization" in LCRP. We discuss budget recipients in each sector as available.

Legal

The legal status of the refugees, to a large extent, determines how they access services in other sectors, including health, education, shelter, and employment, as well as their rights to protection. The current legal status of Syrian refugees in Lebanon and Jordan is tenuous, and the governments have been reluctant to provide durable legal solutions.

While both Jordan and Lebanon have opened their borders and offered their services to the refugees, neither country is a signatory to the 1951 Convention Relating to the Status of Refugees, the international treaty that defines rights of refugees and obligations of states (UNHCR, 2010). This realm is one where the biggest barrier to effective coordination is simply disagreement.

The government of Lebanon has not had a consistent, clear position on the legal status of Syrian refugees. Most of Lebanon's legal rights and responsibilities to refugees originate in the 2003 MOU signed between the government of Lebanon and UNHCR. This document does not allow refugees to apply for permanent asylum status in Lebanon. With respect to Syrian refugees specifically, the controlling document is a bilateral agreement signed between Syria and Lebanon in 1994 (UNHCR, 2003a). According to this agreement, Syrian nationals can enter Lebanon without a visa by showing their national identification card (Di Bartolomeo, Fakhoury, and Perrin, 2010). In order to register for refugee status, Syrians must go through an official border crossing to be granted an entry coupon—free of charge for an initial six-month stay in Lebanon, which can be renewed for free for an additional six months. As of May 2015, UNHCR temporarily suspended new registrations at the request of the government of Lebanon. As a result, individuals who are not included in official counts of registered Syrian refugees in the country are waiting to be registered (UNHCR, 2016a). Without registration, many are unable to access basic services, including health care, education, cash assistance programs, and other provisions. Furthermore, Syrian refugees who registered with UNHCR prior to May 2015 risk losing their limited legal status if they are unable to pay a $200 per-person fee required to renew their registration after their initial 12 months in country (Aranki and Kalis, 2014). These gaps in the registration process have created a legally vulnerable Syrian-refugee population in Lebanon. One refugee interviewed noted that, "We are all illegal. I paid six months ago for a permit, but I cannot afford to renew it."

The government of Jordan signed a MOU with UNHCR in 1998, which adheres to the Convention Relating to the Status of Refugees' definition of a refugee and permits UNHCR to interview "asylum seekers" in Jordan and determine refugee status.[1] While Jordan has not suspended new registration of refugees, their legal status remains tenuous, due to registration policies in particular. Syrians in Jordan receive a 12-month period of temporary protection. The government of Jordan mandated a 30 Jordanian dinar (about $42) health test for renewal of registration. Interviewees criticized this health test as a barrier to refugees' secure legal status, as many refugees cannot afford it and because clinics lack capacity to administer the test in a timely manner to all of the refugees.

UNHCR is the primary UN agency with a mandate to protect refugees and provide registration services. UNHCR's initial legal and protection activities focused on providing temporary protection status to the Syrian refugees, so that they could qualify for services offered by the governments, UN agencies, and NGOs. NGOs provide legal assistance to refugees, work with local governments to improve access to justice, and provide training for national and local authorities on refugee rights and protective standards (International Rescue Committee, 2012, p. 1).

In both countries, gaps within the legal space are significant. Refugees do not understand processes to maintain their registration and legal status, whom to ask for advice, or even whether asking for advice will flag them as having overstayed their legal time allotment. They say that they cannot afford the registration and health-test fees and fear arbitrary arrest and detention. Gaps between legal obligation and actual protection often occur at the local level (with police and local service provision authorities especially) either because local authorities are unaware of their obligations or unwilling to enforce legal protections. One NGO representative described "many contradictions in the legal environment." Previous publications, our interviews, and our focus groups find that the tenuous legal status leaves the refugees at a high risk of exploitation and abuse, including extortion by officials and

---

1 An "informal" copy of this MOU is available online. See "Memorandum of Understanding Between the Government of Jordan and UNHCR," 1998. However, this has been removed from UNHCR's webpage, as there are questions of its legal validity.

employers, arbitrary arrest and detention, and inability to access services (Jacobsen, 2006).

The increased legal vulnerabilities associated with limited protection status differ by gender and age. Because border checkpoints are potentially points of danger for Syrian refugees who entered illegally or have overstayed their initial legal period, more women and children are being sent to work, as they can cross the checkpoints more easily, noted one NGO representative in Lebanon. Men also are more likely to cross into Lebanon illegally by using smugglers and are therefore at more immediate legal risk because they did not cross at an official border. Women are further at risk if they are abandoned by their husbands or, where their marriage was not officially recognized by the state, in the event of a divorce or death (Women's Refugee Commission, 2014).

Discussion of Approach Areas in the Legal/Protection Sector

Short- versus medium-term planning. In both countries, Syrian refugees have a route to temporary legal status, and significant barriers to renewing legal status after a year. Both Lebanon and Jordan also host substantial numbers of Iraqi and Palestinian refugees, also with tenuous legal standing or citizenship rights. In all cases, there has been little interest in planning for the long term in the legal context, with a political preference to view the refugees' stay in Jordan and Lebanon as brief—even when it has already continued for many years.

Parallel versus integrated services. Many refugee legal needs are specific to their status. UNHCR's mandate includes registration of refugees and legal protection under international guidelines. Among other things, this tends to mean pressure on governments to ensure that basic protection is in place and intervening when it appears it is not. These activities are parallel to host-country legal services by definition. Other legal needs, such as registrations of marriages and births or employment disputes, are the same for host-country citizens, yet many interviewees noted that many refugees have difficulty accessing these legal services.

Internationally versus nationally lead. Both international and national actors have substantial leading roles in this sector. The governments of Lebanon and Jordan determine how many refugees are allowed and where registration activities can take place. They have the last say when registration can no longer take place (as is the case in Lebanon in 2015). Meanwhile, UNHCR's mandate is to protect refugees, and therefore it is UNHCR that is responsible for interviewing, vetting, and registering Syrian refugees in both countries.

Focus on refugees versus host communities. UNHCR's mandate is to focus on the refugees. JRP and LCRP request funding for both the refugee-protection mandate of the international community, donor funding for institutional strengthening of national justice systems (with the argument that the Syrians have burdened court capacity), and direct support to citizens of Jordan and Lebanon.

Employment

There was broad consensus among interviewees that access to work is key to enabling solutions in other sectors. Refugees in focus groups in both Lebanon and Jordan identified being able to work as central to addressing many of their survival needs. While there are ongoing calls for greater funding for the refugee crisis, many refugees could support themselves if they could work legally. In many cases, refugees have little alternative but to join the informal economy, where they find themselves with jobs that are illegal, hazardous, exploitative, or poorly paid. The primary challenge here is not coordination but disagreement on goals. Refugees need to work to survive, governments deny legal permission to work in most cases, and the UN and NGOs develop programs to enable employment while using euphemisms to label it as something else, such as "volunteering" or "cash for work."

International standards are meant to ensure rights to employment and livelihoods, both generally (UN, 1948) and for refugees (UNHCR's Agenda for Protection) (UNHCR, 2003b). The 1951 Convention Relating to the Status of Refugees and its 1967 protocol provide further protection for employment, although Lebanon and Jordan are not signatories (Zetter and Ruaudel, 2014). More-specific guidance regarding refugee employment in urban areas is outlined in UNHCR's 2014 publication *Policy on Alternatives to Camps*, which commits to removing obstacles to work, thereby increasing self-reliance (UNHCR, 2014d).

Both Jordan and Lebanon present significant barriers to refugees working; government officials and host communities are fearful of what Syrian competition for jobs means to their own high unemployment rates. While Syrians can apply for work permits in both countries, both government and other stakeholders acknowledged that few refugees are able to obtain them. Reasons include government workers' reticence to process applications, work permit fees for the refugees or employers, security checks (perceived by interviewees as being used to delay work permits), and increasingly complex registration requirements that refugees must meet to obtain a permit.

To date, the Jordanian Ministry of Labor has granted only a small number of work permits: about 800 in the first half of 2015. To address the approximately 160,000 Syrians now working in Jordan (as of August 2014) (Dhingra, 2014; Sadek, 2013, footnote 30), the Ministry of the Interior put in place escalatory punitive measures. They begin with a warning, then progress to a fine. At the next stage, the refugee must sign documentation promising to not work. Finally, refugees may be removed to a camp. Refugees in focus groups described being "caught working," taken to police stations, and forced to sign papers committing to not work. Organizations found employing refugees illegally also incur penalties. A local businessman in Jordan interviewed suggested that an increased number of permits would help to reduce high turnover, exploitation of the Syrians, and risk of penalties for noncompliance. This would help to stabilize the labor market and wages.

The government of Lebanon requires incoming refugees to sign papers stating that they will not work during their stay. While government officials privately claim that penalties for working are not enforced, many refugees said that they fear repercussions and are afraid to work.

These situations make refugees more vulnerable to exploitation and can have distortionary effects on local labor markets. Employers may actually choose to engage refugees rather than citizens, because they can be paid less and are less likely to complain or seek redress if they are treated unfairly (UNHCR, 2009, p. 16). Real or perceived competition for jobs generates tensions with locals. Meanwhile, refugees' alternatives to work, such as sale of assets, are drying up. Many families are relying on negative coping mechanisms like child labor (CARE International, 2014b) and shrinking UN-provided food allowances.

Livelihoods challenges are also gendered (Zetter and Ruaudel, 2014). The pressure to earn a living has implications particularly for adolescent boys sent out to work because of family poverty; they can be subjected to unsafe conditions while working and not in school. Our focus groups in Jordan in particular found that women may find themselves the primary breadwinner in the family due to the comparative ease they have in finding work or when the man in their household was disabled.

Discussion of Approach Areas in the Employment Sector

Short- versus medium-term planning. If a crisis is viewed as short term, work for refugees is not critical, as they can rely on aid to meet their needs. In a more protracted crisis, policies that severely restrict legal employment are not sustainable for refugees. In the current crisis, host-government officials say they are loath to create "pull factors" that keep refugees in their countries. The result is very restrictive laws combined with workarounds to help find employment, such as transportation stipends for volunteering and cash for work, as well as lax enforcement of policies that prohibit work.

Parallel versus integrated services. The refugee crisis in Jordan and Lebanon is creating two parallel labor markets with parallel rules and regulations—a legal labor market for nationals and an illegal and exploitative labor market for refugees.

Internationally versus nationally lead. Employment policies are primarily the responsibility of the governments, although UN agencies and NGOs (mostly international) coordinate work on livelihoods and employment (MOPIC, 2014, and UNOCHA, 2014). Governments restrict legal (or formal) employment, meaning a sizeable proportion of work done by refugees is informal and illegal. International actors in-country tend to provide employment-related programs restricted to vocational training; they provide little in the context of actual work opportunities, in large part due to government restrictions.

Focus on refugees versus host communities. Employment of refugees is controversial due to fears that Syrians (willing to work for less) can take jobs away from citizens, increasing unemployment and reducing wages (Christophersen, Thorleifsson, and Tiltnes, 2013). To date, there have not been comprehensive studies in Jordan or Lebanon about how Syrians can contribute to the local labor markets while not worsening citizen unemployment. Yet there are ways for Syrian labor to be perceived as "win-win." For instance, prior to the crisis, Syrian migrant labor was perceived as the backbone of Lebanon's agricultural economy. Moreover, Syrians could fill gaps in health care and education positions that are needed for the refugees themselves.

Budgets requested for livelihoods in LCRP were $176 million. Much of the funding requested is for job creation and advising for Lebanese workers, as well as vocational training (one interviewee described this as "recreational," given that the refugees cannot work). UN agencies and NGOs also cannot legally hire the refugees. JRP requested $47 million for creating job opportunities for Jordanians. It is not clear why employment is receiving such a large funding request mainly to UN agencies and NGOs. Longer-term employment opportunities for both the refugees and citizens of Jordan and Lebanon will not depend on UN and NGO programs but on local labor markets, labor-market policies, and job skills gained through national education and training facilities. Budget allocations for vocational training raise significant questions about livelihood strategies, since most Syrians cannot obtain work permits; many of the Syrian refugees have job skills if they could legally work; and vocational training is likely to be more effective through Jordanian and Lebanese educational institutions, not NGO programs.

Shelter

Refugees in non-camp settings often rent housing on the open market, whether using their own funds or UNHCR aid (UNHCR, 2014a).

There are substantial difficulties with the housing market for refugees. Affordable and acceptable options are in short supply, forcing refugees to seek suboptimal alternatives. These include multiple families sharing living spaces, informal tented settlements, or makeshift housing (Thorleifsson, 2014, and UNHCR, 2014d). Security of tenure is a particular problem (UNHCR, 2014c). In a survey, up to half of displaced Syrian households had leases that were of uncertain duration or short term (up to six months). These lease arrangements allow landlords to increase rent or evict tenants on short notice and rent to others (whether Syrian or Jordanian) who will pay a higher price (CARE International, 2014). In focus groups, several refugees noted that landlords are often unwilling to sign formal leases, giving the refugees no protection against eviction. Moreover, signed leases are often required as documentation for renewal of registration in Jordan. In both Jordan and Lebanon, the shortfall in housing overall has led to rising rents (MOPIC, 2015a; UNHCR, 2014c). UNHCR (2014d) found that half of the apartments used by refugees are substandard, and informal tented settlements often lack adequate access to water and sanitation.

Gender also affects refugee housing. Female refugees seeking shelter under these conditions face greater risk of sexual and gender-based violence (Women's Refugee Commission, 2014). Women are also more likely to be evicted or exploited, as they obtain written contracts at lower rates than men (UNHCR, 2014c).

Shelter programming for the refugee response has multiple components. Refugees receive shelter assistance in the forms of rental support, direct provision of housing, and upgrades to housing conditions. There are also programs to provide kits for local residents to adapt their homes to enable them to take in refugees (MOPIC, 2015a, and UNHCR, 2014c). A repeatedly mentioned innovative practice is the Norwegian Refugee Council's (NRC's) housing program. NRC provides funding for Jordanian families to renovate their homes in exchange for housing Syrian refugees for a year, to be then replaced by other refugee families. While this invests in the local community's infrastructure and is effective for refugees in the short term, it is not sustainable in the longer term, as refugees need more than one year of shelter.

Activities in the shelter sector are also closely related to those in the sanitation and water sector, as housing and sanitation must be built together (UNHCR, 2014c). Several interviewees mentioned possibly combining the two sectors into a single coordination structure. One aid provider interviewed indicated that the assistance community has not undertaken effective assessments of unmet needs and gaps in the housing sector. Instead, aid providers tend to identify people in substandard conditions on an ad hoc basis.

Discussion of Approach Areas in the Shelter Sector

Short- versus medium-term planning. There are multiple short-term shelter responses, including tents and emergency construction materials (UNHCR, 2016b), shelter caravans (ICRC, 2014), informal tented settlements, subsidies for refugees for rental housing, and assistance with renovations for local homeowners in exchange for their hosting refugees. Many refugees struggle with short-term leases. A longer-term response might include policies that promote and enforce standard leases for refugees, as well as construction of new housing. While investment in infrastructure would imply that the crisis has longevity that governments hesitate to acknowledge, construction could boost local economies.

Parallel versus integrated services. When refugees live in urban areas instead of camps, they access housing that is integrated with the host community. Competition for shelter has been an ongoing cause of tension between hosts and refugees (REACH, 2014, and Fisher, 2014). This may be because areas with large numbers of refugees had experienced rental-price inflation of 100 to 200 percent, fostering an increase in substandard housing for all residents (MOPIC, 2015b). When the influx of refugees drives up rents, low-income Jordanians and Lebanese also suffer.

Internationally versus nationally lead. The shelter sector in Jordan is cochaired by the International Federation of Red Cross and Red Crescent Societies and UNHCR and by UNHCR and UNDP in Lebanon. While housing under non-crisis conditions in urban areas typically involves the private sector, private-sector entities are not involved in shelter coordination.

Focus on refugees versus host communities. Shelter-related funding has elements that are focused on both host communities and on refugees. For instance, while refugees receive rental support, some program providers (e.g., NRC) offer incentives for individual local residents to host refugee families. There has not been a focus on systematically expanding satisfactory housing stock in communities affected by the population increases.

WASH

The refugee crisis has strained the water and sanitation infrastructure of both countries, which, in many cases, was already in need of repair and significant expansion. Areas that experienced rapid population growth because of the refugee crisis are particularly overburdened.

Because WASH activities have been decentralized among national governments, UN agencies, NGOs, and municipalities, there have not been comprehensive assessments of unmet needs and gaps in infrastructure (UN Water and World Health Organization, 2014). The fact that many refugees are scattered throughout informal settlements across Jordan and Lebanon makes identifying needs for rehabilitation of sanitation infrastructure more difficult. This is particularly true in areas such as south Beirut, with its significant Hezbollah presence that discourages foreign intervention, according to interviewees. With informal tented settlements scattered across Lebanon, one UN official said, "WASH is a disaster. Everyone, including donors, underestimates this sector."

A variety of stakeholders are involved in WASH-related coordination, including UNHCR and UNICEF in both Jordan and Lebanon. Over time, the governments took an increasingly active leadership role. A government official in Lebanon said, "There is a lot of confusion in WASH meetings, because sometimes UN agencies don't coordinate with each other, and not with other donors and implementers, and the government." In Lebanon, the Ministry of Energy and Water is the lead agency for this sector, and coordinates—along with MOSA—with host communities about water and sanitation needs. In

Jordan, the Ministry of Water and Irrigation and the Water Authority of Jordan leads water sector governance (MOPIC and UN, 2013).

The WASH sector is somewhat unique in the high level of coordination and interoperability with other sectors that it demands. To deliver clean drinking water, offer sanitary facilities, ensure that there are enough sewage treatment plants, collect garbage, and educate about sanitary practices and health concerns for both the host communities and refugees, WASH activities must be coordinated with shelter-, health-, and education-sector activities. Several of those interviewed from international organizations suggested that WASH should be incorporated in the longer term into one of the other sectors (such as shelter) for both short- and long-term planning and funding purposes.

In Jordan, USAID has been investing in the WASH sector, motivated by the refugee crisis. There are a number of collective and household-level WASH services offered primarily by NGOs: hygiene-promotion programs; environmental hygiene; pregnancy and newborn hygiene; household WASH rehabilitation; and provision of plumbing in housing (ACTED and UNICEF, 2014). However, both NGOs and UN agencies acknowledge the lack of reach of WASH services largely because it is difficult to identify and locate families needing those services, as refugees are diffused within cities and other non-camp areas.

WASH efforts in Lebanon have focused on clean water and habitat in the informal tented settlements, as well as quality of waste services in municipalities. Interviewees from several international organizations expressed frustration that they have been unable to conduct projects that would involve longer-term WASH-infrastructure development in some locations, as doing so would imply that the refugee crisis is not temporary. The Kuwait Fund and the Arab Fund have provided grants to the government of Lebanon's Council for Reconstruction and Development for investment in WASH infrastructure in urban areas and towns.

Discussion of Approach Areas in the WASH Sector

Short versus medium-term planning. To date, WASH planning and funding has largely focused on short-term fixes, without significant long-term infrastructure development, including waste-processing plants and sewage-storage facilities. Such infrastructure plans have been obstructed both by reluctance from donors to make investments in anticipation of a continuing crisis and by government entities that are reticent to create new permanent structures. At the same time, informal tented settlements are becoming increasingly permanent, noted several interviewees. The 2015 3RP prioritizes a "transition from first-phase emergency services to more sustainable and more cost effective systems" for WASH efforts (3RP, 2015a). In the meantime, however, most projects are near-term NGO-delivered efforts.

Parallel versus integrated services. Because integrated WASH projects require a longer-term commitment from governments and donors, refugee assistance has often taken the form of parallel services in distribution of sanitation and hygiene materials, classes on hygiene best practices taught by NGOs, and water delivery. At the same time, WASH infrastructure needs are shared among host communities and refugees.

Internationally versus nationally lead. Government ministries and UN agencies have been involved in the bulk of the high-level strategic planning in this sector. NGOs have largely been responsible for implementing community engagement efforts (Relief International, undated).

Focus on refugees versus host communities. Projects focused on the rehabilitation of existing water or sanitation systems are needed to benefit both refugees and host communities, as water resources are public, shared, and finite, while poor sanitation or waste treatment negatively effects both host and refugee communities.

Health

Health-service access differs in Jordan and Lebanon for refugees because the two countries' health care systems are very different. Health care in Jordan is mainly public, and, in Lebanon, it is highly privatized. In Jordan, public health care was free of charge for registered refugees until 2014. However, due to rising costs and increasing burdens on the system (e.g., hospital beds, specialized consultations), Jordan reduced what it provides for free and began charging for many services.

Lebanon's health care system is highly privatized, which means that many refugees cannot afford it, while efforts to provide it through the aid system have trouble leveraging existing infrastructure (Amnesty International, 2014). In both countries, primary health care services are much more accessible than mental health care and secondary and tertiary health care (which includes specialized treatment for disorders such as epilepsy and cardiac diseases). Barriers to mental health care pose a particular concern, given the needs of Syrian refugees that have resulted from the conflict (WHO, International Medical Corps, Jordanian Ministry of Health, and Eastern Mediterranean Public Health Network, 2013).

In Lebanon, the Ministry of Public Health leads coordination of health care assistance to refugees, in collaboration with the WHO and UNHCR. The ministry lacks capacity to deliver services itself, operating only three primary health care clinics (Dagher, 2013). More than 86 percent of hospital beds in Lebanon are privately owned (Aranki and Kalis, 2014). UNHCR covers the cost of medical appointments for refugees in Lebanon, emphasizing primary and emergency care over more-complex services. Most clinics for refugees are run by local NGOs with the support of international NGOs, and UNICEF supports mobile medical units for emergency demand. The Lebanese medical community is well staffed and well trained, particularly compared with other countries in the region. However, one NGO official noted, there has been no significant attempt to build capacity of national systems to take over management of the health care programs developed by international organizations. Some refugee-response work has focused on building national institutions, such as the Kuwait Fund's assistance for emergency rooms in public hospitals, benefiting both Lebanese and Syrian patients.

Representatives from international organizations believe that the health sector may be the best coordinated in Lebanon. This is perhaps due to strong leadership by the Ministry of Public Health, which requires that organizations working in that sector meet monthly to discuss priorities. At the same time, refugees in focus groups consistently raised health care service gaps as a concern, reporting that they are difficult to access and cost prohibitive, and that information about where to go for primary, secondary, and specialized health care is limited and inconsistent. Moreover, specialized medical care often requires crossing government checkpoints or moving significant distances, both of which incur risk for refugees (Norwegian Refugee Council, 2014). While governmental and international officials feel the systems are functioning properly, the refugees interviewed express discontent with the lack of information, inconsistencies in treatment they experience, and a perceived unwillingness on the part of government officials to interact with them.

In Jordan, the Ministry of Health provides primary, secondary, and tertiary care. While there is an extensive network of primary health care facilities and skilled health workers, the daily workload capacity at public hospitals has increased by 9 to 50 percent, and adverse effects on health services are likely as the crisis continues (Ajlouni, 2014). Still, refugees have been able to access public sector facilities: In a 2014 survey, 85 percent of Syrian refugee households reported that they were able to receive care since their arrival in Jordan (Doocy et al., 2014). As in Lebanon, specialized care or treatment for chronic conditions is significantly more expensive and difficult to attain. In Jordan, the health response has also combined emergency service provision, primarily delivered by NGOs, with capacity-building projects aimed at enhancing the national health system's longer-term ability to absorb the refugee population. Both men and women in refugee focus groups noted that treatment for some medical problems was often cost prohibitive or difficult to physically access.

Discussion of Approach Areas in the Health Sector

Short versus medium-term planning. Health infrastructure is not being developed to increase medium-term sustainability. The focus on temporary emergency and primary health care clinics for Syrian refugees has come at the expense, arguably, of investing in new hospitals and clinics, training new doctors and nurses, and expanding the capacity of Jordanian and Lebanese health systems. Both Lebanon and Jordan have well-trained, capable medical personnel, but the sheer numbers of medical practitioners required in both countries as a result of the crisis has required international experts in the short term. In cases of health care staff shortages, some Syrian refugees with medical training may be an underused resource.

Parallel versus integrated services. Health care provision has largely been run as a parallel service in Lebanon, but has been integrated into public health care in Jordan. Because health care in Lebanon is so privatized, it may not be possible to absorb Syrian refugees into the public health care system; parallel efforts may be needed or, at least, mechanisms (such as insurance) to integrate them into Lebanon's private health care system. In Jordan, integrated public services are under strain, calling either for additional parallel services or expansion of Jordan's health care system capacity.

Internationally versus nationally lead. National leadership of the health care sector has been increasing in both countries. As the crisis has continued, governments have been increasingly active, defining national health policy, where refugees can go to seek treatment, and how funding is distributed to clinics and hospitals. At the same time, international organizations are more flexible, more able to pivot into different project areas and places as needed, and bring capacity that is insufficient in the host countries. As Lebanon's health care system is largely private, there also may be opportunities for greater roles for the private sector with donor support.

Focus on refugees versus host communities. Mental health is a good example of focusing on host communities in ways that also help the refugee community. Mental health has been a successful area of integration and collaboration in Lebanon, with a national mental health program established, driven in part by the refugee crisis.

Education

Refugee kindergarten-through-12th-grade education in both Jordan and Lebanon is under significant strain (Ahmadzadeh et al., 2014, and Culbertson and Constant, 2015). Only one-quarter of Syrian children in Lebanon, and 60 percent in Jordan, are enrolled in formal education. This means that at least 306,000 Syrian children in Lebanon, and 92,000 in Jordan, are not in school (3RP, 2015b).

Syrian refugee children in Jordan and Lebanon access education in several different ways (Culbertson and Constant, 2015). First, both governments made public, formal education available to refugees by integrating refugee children into public classrooms and by opening second shifts in public schools that offer the national curricula. However, even with the double shifting, space and resource shortages remain. This is particularly problematic in Lebanon. Because 70 percent of Lebanese children attend private schools, the public-school system is small. With 275,000 Lebanese children enrolled in public schools, it is not surprising that Lebanon's public-school system has trouble meeting the needs of the 408,000 Syrian children now in the country (Ministry of Education and Higher Education, 2014). To fill gaps, Syrians themselves have opened up schools in Lebanon, although there are little data or understanding about these schools. In both countries, a very small number of Syrians with means send their children to private schools. UN agencies and NGOs operate alternative education programs that offer remedial support (to help keep up in class), catch-up support (to help children who have missed school enter an age-appropriate classroom), and life skills; neither the governments of Jordan nor Lebanon has allowed these programs to offer full-time certified education with pathways to further education or employment.

Barriers to education also include family poverty that forces children to work, trauma, lack of transportation, and lack of programs for children who have been out of school for several years and who are unable to re-enter age-appropriate classrooms (UNICEF, 2013). Gender issues relevant to refugee access to education include greater pressures on boys to earn an income for their households, perceptions among teachers that boys have more trouble in the classroom, early marriage for girls linked to family poverty, and the limited ability of many refugee women and children to leave their homes without an adult male family member.

Coordination of education involves multiple organizations, including governments, UNICEF and UNHCR, and NGOs. In Jordan, UNICEF and Save the Children colead coordination of the education sector (UNHCR, 2016c). In Lebanon, multiple interviewees described how MEHE has taken an increasingly strong leadership role in coordination. In January 2015, MEHE rolled out its Reaching All Children with Education strategy. Controversially, MEHE made government approval of NGO education projects contingent on NGOs falling in line with its new strategy. NGOs found this policy frustrating, because it meant that they could no longer implement programs that they viewed as important based on the circumstances that they saw without approval from MEHE. While some NGOs objected to the new restrictions, several interviewees pointed to it as a model of a host government taking leadership of sector coordination.

Discussion of Approach Areas in the Education Sector

Short- versus medium-term planning. Education responses have focused on increasing access to formal education in Jordan and Lebanon through expansion of double-shifts in existing schools. Education strategies have yet to move to longer-term approaches of expanding capacity to handle greater numbers of children through building additional school buildings, transitioning children from alternative programs to certified programs, or improving quality.

Parallel versus integrated services. In Jordan and Lebanon, about half of Syrian children enrolled in school are educated in the same classrooms as host-country citizens, and half are in Syrian-only classrooms, either through nationality-segregated double shifts or enrollment in NGO- or Syrian-run alternative education. Keeping the communities separated from one another may limit future social cohesion between Syrian and host communities (Culbertson and Constant, 2015). At the same time, capacity limits may necessitate some parallel certified-education structures to meet needs. In Lebanon, because the number of Syrian children needing education exceeds the number of Lebanese children in the public school system, integration and double shifting cannot cover the additional requirements. In Jordan, with a lower ratio of refugee children to host-nation children, expansion of existing public education is more feasible.

Internationally versus nationally lead. In the beginning of the crisis, UN agencies took the lead in coordinating the education responses. In Jordan, UNICEF maintains the coordination lead, while in Lebanon, MEHE has taken leadership of sector coordination. At the same time, formal-education provision is provided by the governments, ensuring a strong government role.

Focus on refugees versus host communities. Education is a source of tension between Syrians and host communities, with citizens frustrated at newly crowded classrooms. Governments have insisted that a third of education assistance goes to programs that support host-country children. USAID and other donors have ongoing programs to invest in school facilities that are beginning to develop links with the refugee response.

Summary

The six sectors we have examined (legal, employment, shelter, WASH, health, and education) vary along the approach areas identified by our framework (time frame, nature of services, leadership, funding recipients, and focus). The differences are represented in Tables A.1 and A.2. These differences highlight how varying priorities of organizations leading the sectors can result in achievement gaps.

Table A.1
Patterns in Jordan's Public-Service Provision to Refugees Across Five Areas

Stakeholder	Time Frame (Short- or Medium-Term)	Services (Parallel or Integrated)	Leadership (International or National)	Funding Recipients (International or National)	Focus (Refugees or Host Communities)
Overarching structure	Short	Both	Both	Both, mostly international	Both
Legal	Short	Parallel	Both	International	Refugees
Employment	Short	Parallel	National	International	Both
Shelter	Short	Integrated	International	International	Refugees
WASH	Medium	Integrated	International	International	Both
Health	Short	Integrated	International	International	Refugees
Education	Short	Both	International	International	Refugees

Table A.2
Patterns in Lebanon's Public-Service Provision to Refugees Across Five Areas

Stakeholder	Time Frame (Short- or Medium-Term)	Services (Parallel or Integrated)	Leadership (International or National)	Funding Recipients (International or National)	Focus (Refugees or Host Communities)
Overarching structure	Short	Both	Both	Mostly international	Both
Legal	Short	Parallel	Both	International	Refugees
Employment	Short	Parallel	National	International	Both
Shelter	Short	Both	International	International	Refugees
WASH	Short	Both	International	Both	Refugees
Health	Short	Parallel	National	Both	Refugees
Education	Short	Both	National	Both	Refugees

There are several key takeaways, as summarized by Tables A.1 and A.2. Most of the sectors in both countries have been dealt with on short-term plans, despite the shift in emphasis to "resilience" and "stabilization." Services are being addressed through a mix of integrated and parallel services. In most cases, a sustainable approach to service provision would involve shifting from UN-supported services to integrated national services. In some cases, there are appropriate reasons for services to remain parallel. These include Lebanon's health, legal, and education sectors, where the public sectors are too small to absorb most of the refugees or where refugees have particular needs (such as in legal protection). Leadership has largely been by international bodies, with increasing levels of government leadership in overarching structures. The governments likely could take further leadership of many sectors, with support, although constraints on institutional capacity may hinder full leadership in coordination. The balance of funding to international bodies (UN agencies and international NGOs) versus to governments seems out of proportion with their responsibilities and the services that they provide. Even where much of the public services are provided by governments, UN agencies and NGOs still manage most of the funding. To date, most programming has focused on refugees as separate entities, as opposed to refugees within the context of their wider host-country communities.

APPENDIX B

Interview and Focus-Group Protocols

Stakeholder Interview Protocol

(Note: The questions were modified according to the expert's sector and country expertise.)

Could you please provide an overview of service provision in our six sectors for refugees in urban areas (1) in general and (2) in Jordan/Lebanon: legal, education, employment, shelter, health, and sanitation.

Who is providing assistance in each of these areas?

What has been particularly effective or innovative in coordination of services to refugees in urban areas? Where are there problems of coordination? Why do you think the things that work, work and those that don't, don't?

What are the biggest challenges and gaps in services? How do they vary by region/locality/other factors? What are the reasons for the gaps (Prompts: No one to provide the services? Lack of access to refugees? Lack of information to refugees? Resource constraints? Fear from the refugees to seek access? Host-country tensions?)

What is working well in international coordination in supporting national authorities? What is not working well? What factors help or hinder coordination? Does it vary by organization/type of organization? If so, how?

Is there substantial duplication of effort in assistance provision? If so, where is it most prevalent/problematical and why do you think it exists?

What are strengths and weaknesses in national or municipal capacities to handle the additional services to refugees?

How could the capacities of local entities be strengthened? (Prompts: national ministries; municipal authorities; local NGOs, community groups, and religious groups.)

What sort of support/coordination takes place between international donors/service providers and national/municipal authorities in providing services to refugees? How does it work?

How do international donors/service providers interact with NGOs, including both donors and service providers?

How is provision of aid and services to refugees typically coordinated with provision of aid and services to urban host communities? Do the same or different people/groups carry these out? How are services specific to refugees provided? What are some services specific to refugees?

Do you perceive tensions between refugees and local populations? If so, does this hamper service provision?

How do refugees access service providing agencies?

How are considerations different for refugees in camps and refugees in urban areas for (your sector)?

Are there considerations specific to particular demographics of urban refugees?

- Male or female or other genders?
- Sexual minorities?

- What about youth refugees?
- Other demographics?
- Do gender, age, or other such factors affect who provides assistance?

What are your views on the effectiveness of resource allocation to refugees:

- in and out of camps
- among sectors
- over time
- to the entities with responsibility for the service provision?

How is the provision of services to refugees evaluated by various organizations you know of? Are standards and measurements similar/compatible?

What do you think are the questions we need to be asking to get at these issues? Whom should we be asking them of? Is there anything that we should have asked but did not?

Explanation and Consent for Focus Group Participation for Refugees

RAND is a nonprofit research institution. We are conducting a study about how Syrian refugees adapt to living in a new city and about how the governments, cities, UN agencies, NGOs, and others can improve management of services for refugees, including shelter, sanitation, health care, education, and employment. The U.S. Department of State is sponsoring the study. The purpose of this project is to support the governments of Jordan and Lebanon and the international humanitarian community in providing services to Syrian refugees in cities.

We are conducting interviews and focus groups to learn about Syrian refugees in urban areas in Jordan and Lebanon. We are speaking with national government officials, city officials, UN agencies, and representatives of NGOs, employers, and community leaders. In addition, we are talking with several groups of refugees to learn about their opinions and experiences.

RAND will use the information you provide for research purposes only. We will not record your name or disclose your identity or other information that would identify you to anyone outside of the project. We will destroy all information that identifies you at the end of the study. However, we would point out that focus group facilitators cannot control whether what is said in focus groups is repeated or shared by other participants. We will ask that everyone respect privacy, but we also ask that you not share anything that you would not want shared outside the session.

Taking part in this focus group is voluntary. Your right to access services is not linked in any way to your decision whether or not to participate. Let us know if you don't want to participate or you want to stop at any time. You should feel free to skip any questions that you prefer not to answer.

Focus Group Protocol for Syrian Refugees in Jordan

Introduction

Can you please tell us about yourself?

- How long in Jordan?
- Occupation?
- Number and type of family members with you in Jordan?

Is this the first place you came to after leaving Syria? How did you arrive in this city? Why did you choose to come to this city? (*Prompts: close to border crossing, job opportunities, other family members present, official instructions, reputation of the city for helping refugees.)*

Who helped you most to get settled when you arrived? (*Prompts: UN agencies, Syrian family members and friends, Jordanian government and city officials, NGOs, other.*)

Who was most effective in helping you access services that you needed? What did they do that was effective?

How did you find information about services and referrals to service providers?

On-Going Service Provision

What are the greatest needs, both met and unmet, for other refugees that you know?

How often do you interact with the following to access services, and how helpful are they in taking care of your needs?

- Jordanian government or city officials
- UN agencies
- Other Syrians (friends, relatives, community groups)
- NGOs

In your opinion, how are refugees' needs being met in the following areas, for individuals, families, and the community?

- Housing
- Health care
- Employment
- Education
- Sanitation services

How does technology help you in meeting your needs in this city? (*Prompts: information from the Internet, mobile or social media; coordination with family and friends about services through technology.*)

What is one thing that could be done to improve how refugees access services that they need?

Closing

What are the biggest challenges for refugee women getting services in this city?

What are the biggest challenges for refugee men getting services in this city?

Are there any other thoughts that you would like to share?

References

3RP—*See* Regional Refugee and Resilience Plan.

Abdih, Yasser, and Carolin Geginat, "The Economic Impact of the Syrian Conflict on Jordan," September 30, 2014. As of November 3, 2014:
http://www.imf.org/external/np/blog/nafida/093014.pdf

ACTED and United Nations Children's Emergency Fund, *ACTED Jordan—WASH Interventions Update, September 2014*, 2014. As of November 12, 2015:
https://data.unhcr.org/syrianrefugees/download.php?id=7166&usg=AFQjCNH0baumMpGHcVhsEZ-k-Qk8mwQ6Lg

ActivityInfo, homepage, undated. As of March 18, 2016:
https://www.activityinfo.org

Ahmadzadeh, Hashem, Metin Çorabatir, Leen Hashem, Jalal Al Husseini, and Sarah Wahby, *Ensuring Quality Education for Young Refugees from Syria (12–25 Years): A Mapping Exercise*, Dawn Chatty, supervisor, Oxford: Refugees Study Centre, Oxford Department of International Development, University of Oxford, September 2014. As of November 12, 2015:
http://www.rsc.ox.ac.uk/files/publications/other/rr-syria-youth-education-2014.pdf

Ajlouni, Musa T., "The Impact of Syrian Refugees on the Health Sector in Jordan," paper presented at the Conference on Syrian Refugees in Jordan: The Question of Society and Media, Kempinski Hotel Dead Sea, Amman, Jordan, December 8–10, 2014.

Amnesty International, *Agonizing Choices: Syrian Refugees in Need of Health Care in Lebanon*, 2014. As of November 12, 2015:
https://www.amnesty.org/download/Documents/8000/mde180012014en.pdf

Aranki, Dalia, and Olivia Kalis, *Limited Legal Status for Refugees from Syria in Lebanon, Forced Migration Review*, September 2014.

Buchanan-Smith, Margaret, and Simon Maxwell, "Linking Relief and Development: An Introduction and Overview," *IDS Bulletin,* Vol. 25, No. 4, October 1994. As of November 3, 2015:
http://www.eldis.org/fulltext/LinkingReliefandDevelopment.pdf

CARE International, *Lives Unseen: Urban Syrian Refugees and Jordanian Host Communities Three Years into the Syria Crisis*, Amman, Jordan: April 15, 2014a. As of October 27, 2015:
http://reliefweb.int/report/jordan/lives-unseen-urban-syrian-refugees-and-jordanian-host-communities-three-years-syria

———, "International Day Against Child Labour: Child Labour Among Syrian Refugees Rises With Every Day the Crisis Continues," June 5, 2014b. As of March 18, 2016:
http://reliefweb.int/report/jordan/international-day-against-child-labour-child-labour-among-syrian-refugees-rises-every

Christophersen, Mona, Cathrine Moe Thorleifsson, and Åge A. Tiltnes, *Ambivalent Hospitality: Coping Strategies and Local Responses to Syrian Refugees in Lebanon*, Oslo, Norway: Fafo AIS, 2013. As of October 28, 2014:
http://www.fafo.no/index.php/nb/zoo-publikasjoner/fafo-rapporter/item/ambivalent-hospitality

Cox, Simon, "The Billion-Dollar Aid Question," BBC Radio 4, October 27, 2015. http://www.bbc.co.uk/programmes/b06kch0m

Crisp, Jeff, Greg Garras, Jenny McAvoy, Ed Schenkenberg, Paul Spiegel, and Frances Voon, *From Slow Boil to Breaking Point: A Real-Time Evaluation of UNHCR's Response to the Syrian Refugee Emergency*, PDES/2013/13, Geneva, Switzerland: United Nations High Commissioner for Refugees, July 2013. As of April 14, 2016:
http://www.unhcr.org/52b83e539.html

Culbertson, Shelly, and Louay Constant, *Education of Syrian Refugee Children: Managing the Crisis in Turkey, Lebanon, and Jordan*, Santa Monica, Calif.: RAND Corporation, 2015, RR-859-CMEPP. As of November 24, 2015:
http://www.rand.org/pubs/research_reports/RR859.html

Dagher, Diana, *Challenges in Delivering Health Care for Syrian Refugees in Lebanon*, Los Angeles: International Medical Corps, 2013. As of November 12, 2015:
https://internationalmedicalcorps.org/document.doc?id=293

Dhingra, Reva, "Syrian Refugees and the Jordanian Economy," *Muftah*, August 21, 2014. As of November 12, 2015:
http://muftah.org/syrian-refugees-jordanian-economy/#.VKqX_fNFB9A

Di Bartolomeo, Anna, Tamirace Fakhoury, and Delphine Perrin, *CARIM—Migration Profile: Lebanon*, Florence, Italy: Euro-Mediterranean Consortium for Applied Research on International Migration, Robert Schuman Centre for Advanced Studies, European University Institute, January 2010. http://www.carim.org/public/migrationprofiles/MP_Lebanon_EN.pdf

Doocy, Shannon, Emily Lyles, Timothy Robertson, William Weiss, and Gilbert Burnham, *Syrian Refugee Health Access Survey in Jordan*, the Center for Refugee and Disaster Response at Johns Hopkins University Bloomberg School of Public Health, the World Health Organization, the School of Nursing at Jordan University for Science and Technology, the United Nations High Commissioner for Refugees, and the Ministry of Health of the Hashemite Kingdom of Jordan, December 2014.

Easterly, William, and Tobias Pfutze, "Where Does the Money Go? Best and Worst Practices in Foreign Aid," *Journal of Economic Perspectives,* Vol. 22, No. 2, Spring 2008. As of March 18, 2016:
https://www.ciaonet.org/attachments/907/uploads

Feinstein International Center, *Refugee Livelihoods in Urban Areas: Identifying Program Opportunities*, October 2012. As of April 10, 2014:
http://fic.tufts.edu/publication-item/refugee-livelihoods-in-urban-areas-identifying-program-opportunities/

Financial Tracking Service, "Total Funding to the Syrian Crisis 2015," 2016. As of April 5, 2016:
https://fts.unocha.org/pageloader.aspx?page=special-syriancrisis&year=2015

Fisher, Nigel, "Foreword: The Inheritance of Loss," *Forced Migration Review,* Vol. 47, September 2014. As of October 24, 2014:
http://www.fmreview.org/syria/fisher

Grant, Harriet, "UN Agencies 'Broke and Failing' in Face of Ever-Growing Refugee Crisis," *Guardian*, September 6, 2015. As of November 12, 2015:
http://www.theguardian.com/world/2015/sep/06/refugee-crisis-un-agencies-broke-failing

Harvey, Paul, and Jeremy Lind, *Dependency and Humanitarian Relief: A Critical Analysis*, HPG Report 19, London: Humanitarian Policy Group at Overseas Development Institute, July 2005. As of November 3, 2015:
http://www.odi.org.uk/hpg/papers/HPGreport19.pdf

Hashemite Kingdom of Jordan, Ministry of Planning and International Cooperation, *Final Draft National Resilience Plan 2014–2016: Proposed Priority Responses to Mitigate the Impact of the Syrian Crisis on Jordan and the Jordanian Host Communities*, June 19, 2014. As of March 18, 2016:
http://static1.squarespace.com/static/522c2552e4b0d3c39ccd1e00/t/53f300ffe4b082b86e9e72bd/1408434431620/NRP_FinalDraft_June2014.pdf

———, "Jordan Response Plan for the Syria Crisis: Executive Summary, 2015," 2015a. As of January 28, 2015:
https://docs.unocha.org/sites/dms/Syria/Jordan%20Response%20Plan.pdf

———, "JORISS JRP 2015 Funding Update," May 13, 2015b.
http://static1.squarespace.com/static/522c2552e4b0d3c39ccd1e00/t/555488dde4b0234e02cb8e9f/1431603421577/JORISS+JRP+Funding+Update_2015.05.14.pdf

Hashemite Kingdom of Jordan, Ministry of Planning and International Cooperation, and the United Nations, *Needs Assessment Review of the Impact of the Syrian Crisis on Jordan*, Host Community Support Platform, November 2013. As of November 12, 2015:
http://www.undp.org/content/dam/rbas/doc/SyriaResponse/Jordan%20Needs%20Assessment%20-%20November%202013.pdf

———, *Jordan Response Plan for the Syria Crisis: Annexes, March 2015*, March 31, 2015. As of March 28, 2016:
http://reliefweb.int/report/jordan/jordan-response-plan-2015-syria-crisis-march-2015-enar

Hidalgo, Silvia, Dorian LaGuardia, Gabriella Trudi, Ricardo Sole, Ziad Moussa, Jolanda van Dijk, Peter Merckx, and Lena Zimmer, *Independent Programme Evaluation (IPE) of UNHCR's Response to the Refugee Influx in Lebanon and Jordan*, Brussels, Belgium: Transtec S.A., January 29, 2015. As of November 12, 2015:
http://www.unhcr.org/5551f5c59.pdf

Humanitarian Response, "What Is the Cluster Approach?" undated. As of April 18, 2016:
https://www.humanitarianresponse.info/en/coordination/clusters/what-cluster-approach

ICRC—*See* International Committee of the Red Cross.

Implementation of the Intergovernmental Sustainable Development Agenda, "News: UN Prepares for Summit on Refugees and Migrants," January 5, 2016. As of March 18, 2016:
http://sd.iisd.org/news/un-prepares-for-summit-on-refugees-and-migrants/

International Committee of the Red Cross, "Jordan: More Syrian Refugees Seeking Shelter," August 28, 2014. As of January 2, 2015:
https://www.icrc.org/en/document/jordan-more-syrian-refugees-seeking-shelter#.VKacBPNFD5o

International Rescue Committee, "Urban Refugees: From Harm to Home," November 2012. As of November 12, 2015:
http://www.rescue-uk.org/sites/default/files/20.11.12%20Urban%20refs%20for%20ECHO%20advocacy%20event%20_0.pdf

Jacobsen, Karen, "Refugees and Asylum Seekers in Urban Areas: A Livelihoods Perspective," *Journal of Refugee Studies,* Vol. 19, No. 3, 2006, pp. 273–286.

The Jordan Response Platform for the Syria Crisis, "Jordan Response Plan 2015 Financial Tracking," 2015a. As of March 18, 2016:
http://www.jrpsc.org/jrpfts/

———, "JORISS 4W Activity Search—English," 2015b. As of March 18, 2016:
http://www.jrpsc.org/4wactivityen

Kumar, Isabelle, "King Abdullah: ISIL 'A War Inside of Islam' That We Need to Fight Together," *Euronews*, November 11, 2015. As of November 12, 2015: http://www.euronews.com/2015/11/11/exclusive-king-abdullah-ii-on-syrian-refugees-in-jordan-and-the-islamic-state/

Landau, Loren B., "Protection as Capability Expansion: Practical Ethics for Assisting Urban Refugees," in David Hollenbach, ed., *Refugee Rights: Ethics, Advocacy, and Africa*, Washington, D.C.: Georgetown University Press, 2008, pp. 103–121.

Luck, Taylor, "In Jordan, Tensions Rise Between Syrian Refugees and Host Community," *Washington Post*, April 21, 2013. As of November 3, 2015: https://www.washingtonpost.com/world/middle_east/in-jordan-tensions-rise-between-syrian-refugees-and-host-community/2013/04/21/d4f5fa24-a762-11e2-a8e2-5b98cb59187f_story.html

"Memorandum of Understanding Between the Government of Jordan and UNHCR," in Arabic and English, April 5, 1998. As of November 12, 2015: http://www.carim.org/public/legaltexts/LE2JOR002_AREN.pdf

Ministry of Education and Higher Education, *Reaching All Children with Education in Lebanon (R.A.C.E.)*, June 2014. As of March 18, 2016: http://www.mehe.gov.lb/uploads/file/2015/Feb2015/Projects/RACEfinalEnglish2.pdf

MOPIC—*See* Hashemite Kingdom of Jordan, Ministry of Planning and International Cooperation.

Morand, MaryBeth, Katherine Mahoney, Shaula Bellour, and Janice Rabkin, *The Implementation of UNHCR's Policy on Refugee Protection and Solutions in Urban Areas: Global Survey—2012*, Geneva, Switzerland: United Nations High Commissioner for Refugees, 2013. As of March 18, 2016: http://www.unhcr.org/516d658c9.pdf

Moussaouri, Rana, "Paralysed Lebanon Government Risks Losing Millions in Aid," Yahoo News, November 1, 2015. As of November 1, 2015. http://news.yahoo.com/paralysed-lebanon-government-risks-losing-millions-aid-115907764.html

Norwegian Refugee Council, *The Consequences of Limited Legal Status for Syrian Refugees in Lebanon: NRC Lebanon Field Assessment, Part Two: North, Bekaa, and South*, March 2014. As of March 21, 2016: https://data.unhcr.org/syrianrefugees/download.php?id=5235

OECD—*See* the Organization for Economic Coordination and Development.

Organization for Economic Coordination and Development, *International Support to Post-Conflict Transition: Rethinking Policy, Changing Practice*, DAC Guidelines and Reference Series, Paris: OECD Publishing, 2012. As of March 18, 2016: http://www.keepeek.com/Digital-Asset-Management/oecd/development/international-support-to-post-conflict-transition_9789264168336-en#page1

Palagashvili, Liya, and Claudia R. Williamson, "Ranking Foreign Aid Agency Best Practices: New Donors, New Findings," working paper, 2014.

"Prince El-Hassan: Syrian Refugees Crisis Requires National-Level Thinking," Ammon News, December 7, 2014. As of January 20, 2015:
http://en.ammonnews.net/article.aspx?articleno=27251#.VJlCqV4BA

Rainey, Venetia, "Lebanon: No Formal Refugee Camps for Syrians," *Al Jazeera*, March 11, 2015. As of November 3, 2015:
http://www.aljazeera.com/news/2015/03/lebanon-formal-refugee-camps-syrians-150310073219002.html

REACH, *Livelihoods, Employment and Tensions in Jordanian Communities Hosting Syrian Refugees, Thematic Assessment Report*, June 30, 2014. As of March 18, 2016:
http://reliefweb.int/sites/reliefweb.int/files/resources/REACH_JOR_Report_EmploymentandTensionsinJordanianCommunitiesHostingSyrianRefugees.pdf

Regional Refugee and Resilience Plan, *Regional Refugee and Resilience Plan 2015–2016 in Response to the Syria Crisis: Regional Strategic Overview*, March 2015a. As of January 28, 2015:
http://www.3rpsyriacrisis.org/wp-content/uploads/2015/01/3RP-Report-Overview.pdf

———, *Regional Quarterly Update: 3RP Achievements—March 2015*, 3RP Regional Refugee and Resilience Plan 2015–2016, March 2015b. As of January 28, 2015:
http://www.3rpsyriacrisis.org/wp-content/uploads/2015/06/3RP-Regional-Dashboards-March-2015.pdf

———, *Funding Snapshot—Top Donor Group Meeting, September 2015*, 3RP Regional Refugee and Resilience Plan 2015–2016, September 2015c. As of November 3, 2015:
http://www.3rpsyriacrisis.org/wp-content/uploads/2015/09/3RP-Funding-Snapshot.pdf

Relief International, "Jordan: Improving Water, Sanitation, and Hygiene (WASH) in Schools," undated. As of March 28, 2016:
https://web.archive.org/web/20151008015405/http://www.ri.org/story.php?ID=136

Ronald, Christopher, *Costs and Benefits of Coordination of United Nations Operational Activities for Development: A Background Paper Prepared for DESA*, April 2011. As of November 12, 2015:
http://www.un.org/esa/coordination/pdf/final_report_2011.pdf

Sadek, George, *Legal Status of Refugees: Egypt, Jordan, Lebanon, and Iraq*, Washington, D.C.: The Law Library of Congress, Global Legal Research Center, December 2013. As of January 5, 2015:
http://www.loc.gov/law/help/refugees/legal-status-refugees.php#_ftn30

Sharp, Jeremy M., *Jordan: Background and U.S. Relations*, Washington, D.C.: Congressional Research Service, RL33546, January 27, 2016. As of March 18, 2016:
https://www.fas.org/sgp/crs/mideast/RL33546.pdf

Slaughter, Amy, and Jeff Crisp, *A Surrogate State?: The Role of UNHCR in Protracted Refugee Situations,* Geneva, Switzerland: Policy Development and Evaluation Service, United Nations High Commissioner for Refugees, January 2009. As of March 18, 2016:
http://www.unhcr.org/4981cb432.html

Thorleifsson, Cathrine, "Coping Strategies Among Self-Settled Syrians in Lebanon," *Forced Migration Review,* Vol. 47, September 2014. As of October 28, 2014:
http://www.fmreview.org/en/syria/thorleifsson.pdf

Trading Economics, "GNI Per Capita—PPP (US Dollar) in Syria," March 18, 2016. As of March 18, 2016:
http://www.tradingeconomics.com/syria/gni-per-capita-ppp-us-dollar-wb-data.html

UN—*See* United Nations.

UN Water, and World Health Organization, "Jordan: Sanitation, Drinking-Water and Hygiene Status Overview," 2014. As of November 12, 2015:
http://www.who.int/water_sanitation_health/glaas/2014/jor_jordan_en.pdf

UNHCR—*See* United Nations High Commissioner for Refugees.

UNICEF—*See* United Nations Children's Emergency Fund.

United Nations, *The Universal Declaration of Human Rights*, December 10, 1948. As of October 14, 2015:
http://www.un.org/en/documents/udhr/index.shtml

United Nations Children's Emergency Fund, *Handbook for Coordinating Gender-Based Violence Interventions in Humanitarian Settings*, Gender-based Violence Area of Responsibility Working Group (GBV AoR), 2010. As of November 12, 2015:
http://www.unicef.org/protection/files/GBV_Handbook_Long_Version.pdf

———, *Shattered Lives: Challenges and Priorities for Syrian Children and Women in Jordan*, Amman, Jordan, June 2013. As of July 2014:
http://www.unicef.org/infobycountry/files/Shattered_Lives_June10.pdf

United Nations High Commissioner for Refugees, "Good Practices for Urban Refugees: Database for Professionals Working with Urban Refugees," undated(a). As of March 21, 2016:
http://www.urbangoodpractices.org

———, "Refugee Assistance Information System (RAIS)," undated(b). As of March 18, 2016:
http://raisunhcr.org

———, "Shelter: A Roof Over Their Heads," undated(c). As of March 18, 2016:
http://www.unhcr.org/pages/49c3646cf2.html

———, "Country Operations Plan—Country: Lebanon," September 2003a. As of March 18, 2016:
http://www.unhcr.org/refworld/pdfid/3fd9c6a14.pdf

———, *Agenda for Protection*, Geneva, Switzerland, October 2003b. As of March 25, 2016:
http://www.unhcr.org/3e637b194.html

———, "UNHCR Policy on Refugee Protection and Solutions in Urban Areas," September 2009. As of January 7, 2015:
http://www.refworld.org/docid/4ab8e7f72.html

———, *Convention and Protocol Relating to the Status of Refugees*, text of the 1951 Convention Relating to the Status of Refugees, text of the 1967 Protocol Relating to the Status of Refugees, and Resolution 2198 (XXI) adopted by the United Nations General Assembly, Geneva, Switzerland, December 2010. As of November 12, 2015:
http://www.unhcr.org/3b66c2aa10.html

———, *Ensuring Access to Education: Operational Guidance on Refugee Protection and Solutions in Urban Areas*, Geneva, Switzerland, 2011a. As of January 14, 2015:
http://www.unhcr.org/4ea9552f9.html

———, *Ensuring Access to Health Care: Operational Guidance on Refugee Protection and Solutions in Urban Areas*, Geneva, Switzerland, 2011b. As of November 12, 2015:
http://www.unhcr.org/4e26c9c69.html

———, *Promoting Livelihoods and Self-Reliance: Operational Guidance on Refugee Protection and Solutions in Urban Areas*, Geneva, Switzerland, 2011c. As of April 9, 2014:
http://www.unhcr.org/cgi-bin/texis/vtx/home/opendocPDFViewer.html?docid=4eeb19f49&query=promoting%20livelihoods%20and%20self-reliance

———, *UNHCR Global Trends 2010*, Geneva, Switzerland, 2011d. As of November 12, 2015:
http://www.unhcr.org/4dfa11499.html

———, *2014 Syria Regional Response Plan: Jordan*, Geneva, Switzerland, 2014a. As of January 2, 2015:
http://www.unhcr.org/syriarrp6/docs/syria-rrp6-jordan-response-plan.pdf

———, *Policy on Alternatives to Camps*, Geneva, Switzerland, 2014b. As of January 2, 2015:
http://www.unhcr.org/5422b8f09.pdf

———, *Syria Regional Response Plan, Jordan: Mid-Year Update*, 2014c. As of January 6, 2015:
http://www.unhcr.org/syriarrp6/midyear/docs/syria-rrp6-myu-jordan.pdf

———, *Syrian Refugees Living Outside Camps in Jordan: Home Visit Data Findings, 2013*, Amman, Jordan, 2014d. As of January 2, 2015:
http://rfg.ee/upYs5

———, *UNHCR Global Trends 2013: War's Human Cost*, Geneva, Switzerland, June 20, 2014e. As of January 14, 2015:
http://www.unhcr.org/5399a14f9.html

———, "Jordan Inter-Agency Operational Update," September–October 2014f. As of November 2014:
http://www.unhcr.org/5465c15d9.html

———, "Introducing the Vulnerability Assessment Framework," December 2014g. As of November 12, 2015:
http://data.unhcr.org/syrianrefugees/download.php?id=7877

———, "2015 UNHCR Country Operations Profile—Jordan," 2015a. As of March 18, 2016:
http://www.unhcr.org/pages/49e486566.html

———, "Refugee Response Coordination Structure," February 2015b. As of March 18, 2016:
http://data.unhcr.org/jordan/coordination.html

———, *UNHCR Global Trends: Forced Displacement in 2014*, Geneva, Switzerland, June 18, 2015c. As of July 24, 2015:
http://unhcr.org/556725e69.html

———, "Syria Regional Refugee Response: Lebanon (Interagency Information Sharing Portal)," January 31, 2016a. As of November 3, 2015:
http://data.unhcr.org/syrianrefugees/country.php?id=122

———, "Syria Regional Refugee Response: Jordan (Total Persons of Concern)," March 16, 2016b. As of November 3, 2015:
http://data.unhcr.org/syrianrefugees/country.php?id=107

———, "Syria Regional Refugee Response: Regional Overview," March 16, 2016c. As of November 3, 2015:
http://data.unhcr.org/syrianrefugees/regional.php

———, "Syria Regional Refugee Response: Zaatari Refugee Camp (Total Persons of Concern)," March 16, 2016d. As of November 3, 2015:
http://data.unhcr.org/syrianrefugees/settlement.php?id=176&country=107&region=77

United Nations Office for the Coordination of Humanitarian Affairs, "Cluster Coordination," undated(a). As of March 18, 2016:
http://www.unocha.org/what-we-do/coordination-tools/cluster-coordination

———, homepage, undated(b). As of March 18, 2016:
http://www.unocha.org

———, "Humanitarian Bulletin: Syria," Issue 01, June 5, 2012. As of March 19, 2015:
http://reliefweb.int/sites/reliefweb.int/files/resources/Full_doc_37.pdf

———, *Lebanon Crisis Response Plan 2015–16*, 2014. As of November 12, 2015:
https://docs.unocha.org/sites/dms/CAP/2015-2016_Lebanon_CRP_EN.pdf

———, "Syrian Arab Republic," 2015. As of March 18, 2016:
http://www.unocha.org/syria

United Nations Relief and Works Agency for Palestine Refugees in the Near East, "What We Do: Education," undated. As of November 3, 2015:
http://www.unrwa.org/what-we-do/education

———, "Where We Work: Lebanon," 2015. As of November 3, 2015:
http://www.unrwa.org/where-we-work/lebanon

The United States Mission to the United Nations, "UN Transparency and Accountability Initiative," undated. As of March 21, 2016:
http://usun.state.gov/about/2196/6657

UNOCHA—*See* United Nations Office for the Coordination of Humanitarian Affairs.

UNRWA—*See* United Nations Relief and Works Agency for Palestine Refugees in the Near East.

"The Urban Challenge for Refugees," IRIN: The Inside Story on Emergencies, January 9, 2013. As of March 18, 2016:
http://www.irinnews.org/report/97203/the-urban-challenge-for-refugees

"Where Does UK Aid to Syria Actually Go?," *BBC News*, October 27, 2015. As of November 12, 2015:
http://www.bbc.com/news/magazine-34636312

WHO—*See* World Health Organization.

Women's Refugee Commission, *Unpacking Gender: The Humanitarian Response to the Syrian Refugee Crisis in Jordan*, March 2014. As of November 12, 2015:
https://womensrefugeecommission.org/resources/233-gender-issues/985-unpacking-gender-the-humanitarian-response-to-the-syrian-refugee-crisis-in-jordan

World Bank, "Country and Lending Groups," undated(a). As of March 18, 2016:
http://data.worldbank.org/about/country-and-lending-groups

———, "Population, Total," undated(b). As of January 28, 2015:
http://data.worldbank.org/indicator/SP.POP.TOTL

———, *Africa Development Indicators 2012/13*, Washington, D.C., 2013. As of March 17, 2014:
https://openknowledge.worldbank.org/bitstream/handle/10986/13504/9780821396162.pdf?sequence=1

World Food Programme, *Vulnerability Assessment of Syrian Refugees in Lebanon*, 2013. As of November 12, 2015:
http://data.unhcr.org/syrianrefugees/download.php?id=3853

World Health Organization, International Medical Corps, Jordanian Ministry of Health, and Eastern Mediterranean Public Health Network, *Assessment of Mental Health and Psychosocial Support Needs of Displaced Syrians in Jordan*, July 2013. As of November 12, 2015:
http://www.urban-response.org/resource/19462

Zetter, Roger, and George Deikun, "Meeting Humanitarian Challenges in Urban Areas," *Forced Migration Review,* Vol. 34, No. 6, February 2010, pp. 5–7. As of April 10, 2014:
http://reliefweb.int/sites/reliefweb.int/files/resources/6F798FB43C30FEF54925770200227E80-FMR_feb2010.pdf

Zetter, Roger, and Héloïse Ruaudel, "Development and Protection Challenges of the Syrian Refugee Crisis," *Forced Migration Review,* Vol. 47, September 2014. As of October 24, 2014:
http://www.fmreview.org/syria/contents